THE 20% DOCTRINE

THE 20% DOCTRINE

HOW TINKERING, GOOFING OFF, AND BREAKING THE RULES AT WORK DRIVE SUCCESS IN BUSINESS

RYAN TATE

HARPER
BUSINESS

An Imprint of HarperCollinsPublishers
www.harpercollins.com

HarperCollins books may be purchased for educational, business, or sales promotional use. For information, please write: Special Markets Department, HarperCollins Publishers, 10 East 53rd Street, New York, NY 10022.

FIRST EDITION

Designed by Renato Stanisic

Library of Congress Cataloging-in-Publication Data has been applied for.

ISBN: 978-0-06-200323-2

12 13 14 15 16   OV/RRD   10 9 8 7 6 5 4 3 2 1

CONTENTS

FOREWORD

by Chad Dickerson

On December 12, 2005, the phone at my desk rang. It was the Yahoo HR department. The phone at my desk almost never rang, so this was a bit of a surprise. I had just helped put together something really awesome, though, so I smiled and braced myself for a hearty congratulations.

The Friday before, I had organized the first internal Hack Day at Yahoo with the help of a loosely organized band of people around the company. The "hack" designation for the day was a tip of the hat to hacker culture, but also a nod to the fact that we were trying to fix a system that didn't work particularly well. The idea was really simple: All the engineers in our division were given the day off to build anything they wanted to build. The only rules were to build something in a twenty-four-hour period and then show it at the end. The basic structure of the event itself was inspired by what we had seen at small startups, but no one had attempted such an event on a large scale and at an established company.

The first Yahoo! Hack Day was clearly a success. In a company that was struggling to innovate, about seventy prototypes appeared out of nowhere in a single twenty-four-hour period, and they were presented in a joyfully enthusiastic environment in which people whooped and yelled and cheered. Sleep-deprived, T-shirt-clad developers stayed late at work on a Friday night to show prototypes they had built for no other reason than they wanted to build something. In his seminal book about open-source software, *The Cathedral and the Bazaar*, Eric Raymond wrote, "Every good work of software starts by scratching a developer's personal itch." There clearly had been a lot of developer itching around Yahoo, but it took Hack Day to let them issue a collective cathartic scratch.

But back to that call from HR. I grabbed the phone, prepared to be gracious, then the HR person on the other end told me we needed to take down one of the hacks, by Cal Henderson, who had created an application program interface, or API, to our company directory (available on Yahoo's intranet, known as "Backyard") and built a hot-or-not-style "Backyard War" app on top of it. No one was ever really sure what these wars were about, but it was viscerally fun to place random coworkers in battle with one another over unknown stakes. The impromptu judging committee I had put together had given Cal a trophy for his work.

The HR person who called me had made a critical error in reasoning. While I had organized Hack Day, I by no means had any actual control over the event itself or any of the participants. I had designed it that way. There were no sign-ups in advance, no proscribed projects or areas of focus, and no central servers where the projects lived. I couldn't have taken Backyard

War down if I'd had a gun to my head. In the end, I think HR may have eventually gotten to Cal, but it didn't matter. At future Hack Days, there was always a feeling of danger, and although no one ever really said it, there was an ongoing secret competition to see who would get the call from HR this time. When you're trying to get things done and change a system, expect to upset a few people along the way.

With that first event, the die was cast, and the completely improvised format from that first Hack Day became something of a standard. At that first Hack Day, I didn't expect seventy presentations (remember, I had no idea who was presenting until they got started). I had originally planned to give each team five to ten minutes to present, but with seventy hacks, I called an audible—each presentation would be two minutes or less. Years later, I found myself in an elevator at the site of a Hack Day and heard one hacker explaining the rules to another: "Dude, demos are always two minutes. It's a rule." I chuckled to myself that these "rules" had become so solidified over time.

After that, we did Hack Days all over the world, on three continents. We continued doing internal ones for employees, and did our first open one for the public nine months after the first internal one. The basic "rules" remained. People built huge numbers of prototypes to solve a wide range of problems, and the only thing that really changed from place to place was the food. We had pizza in California, samosas in Bangalore, and bad English pizza in London.

In London, we did a joint Hack Day with the BBC and held it at Alexandra Palace. Just after the event started, lightning struck and the power went out, triggering a fire-suppression system that opened up large sections of the roof, causing indoor rain. Hackers pulled out umbrellas and simply started drawing on paper until the power came back. Once the creative spirit reaches liftoff, even an unexpected indoor rainstorm just isn't enough to stop it.

Since that first Hack Day, there have been Hack Days at companies like IBM. GroupMe was born at the Techcrunch Disrupt Hack Day in May 2010, funded three months later, then sold for tens of millions of dollars within a year. Hack days are being organized by government agencies to help citizens improve government. Just recently, LinkedIn organized a Hack Day to help veterans.

People ask me all the time why Hack Days work so well. The secret of Hack Day is pretty simple: Doing something is the only thing that matters at a Hack Day. You can have the best idea in the world, but if you can't put some meat on it, no one cares. When I organized the first one, Yahoo had something internally called "Idea Factory," a sophisticated online suggestion box to capture ideas from people around the company. Capturing ideas in such a way sounds perfectly innocuous, but such a system has a key ideological flaw: It anticipates that someone else is going to take your idea and do something with it, relieving you of all responsibility (except, as I learned, complaining that no one had used your awesome idea yet). Hack day solves that problem. You're responsible for idea and execution, and your two minutes better have a demo or you're toast.

Hack Days separate doers from talkers. In the communications around that first Hack Day, I had thrown in a "no PowerPoint" directive to protect the event from the pernicious scourge of corporate slide decks, and that became a rallying cry. There simply was no place for the dull corporate drone of bland PowerPoints. Occasionally, someone would try to present a PowerPoint without a prototype. Without fail, that person would be roundly booed and ruthlessly cut off if he didn't step away willingly. The cultural norms of Hack Day simply did not allow for vacuous grandstanding. Stop talking and show me what you built. We've only got two minutes.

In this book, you will learn about the many ways different organizations have tried to innovate, and you can bet they all share this: They trust that people will do awesome things when given room to do it, and they take great pains to create that room.

Happy hacking, and remember that you don't really have to answer the phone when HR calls.

THE 20% DOCTRINE

INTRODUCTION

Gary Hamel had been a business school professor for nearly twenty-five years when the ego-pummeling epiphany came to him: His kind weren't of much use. Students trained in the best management innovations weren't the best managers of innovation. In some cases, business school training was actively harmful.

Hamel had just completed an investigation of Google, interviewing the Internet company's top executives, charting its history, and obsessively probing how its employees delivered a stream of world-changing products. He spent time with then-CEO Eric Schmidt, met with middle managers, and went into the trenches to talk to rank-and-file employees. His big insight came as he was writing up his case study for the Harvard School of Business, recounting in amazement how Google seemed perpetually on the "brink of chaos," how its "20 percent time" policy fed an orgy of personal experimentation and a slew of innovative, and sometimes quite profitable, new business lines. In a world where the pace of change was relentless, Google was one of the few businesses that could keep up.

Hamel couldn't help but notice that Google was built to avoid managers like the ones he educated. MBA holders are supposed to catalyze and direct change. But Googlers were barely supervised, with managers spread over a "wafer thin" hierarchy, as Hamel put it. And not one of Google's ruling troika, including Schmidt and cofounders Sergey Brin and Larry Page, had a management degree. Nor did the other business leaders Hamel admired, like Whole Foods CEO John Mackey.

"Did you notice?" Hamel asked in his case study. "Mackey, Bill Gore [inventor of Gore-Tex], Sergey Brin, and Larry Page—none of these management innovators went to business school. This is a bit humbling for someone like me who's been a b-school professor for a quarter of a century, but there's no way around it. When you go to business school, you get a lot of wisdom, but you get a lot of dogma, too.

"On the other hand, anyone can learn how to challenge conventional wisdom. . . . The people with the boldest and most useful ideas about how to reinvent your company's core management process are probably not the folks who are managing those processes right now.

"Management innovators should take a lot of advice from people who've never learned what they're not supposed to do."

Hamel is not the only one in American business having a humbling moment right now. The old ways don't seem to be working. Granted, there are bright spots, particularly in the unconventional tech sector, as Hamel noticed. And the economy has, technically speaking, emerged from recession, into a disconcertingly shaky "recovery." But more than three years after the financial system melted down, smaller businesses are still having a tough time getting financing, according to the Treasury Department, while large companies are shunned by individual stock investors, who, on balance, have continued to pull money out of domestic stock funds. Business investment on equipment and plant remains worrisomely close to its recent forty-year low. And hiring has been anemic; unemployment has remained stubbornly near 9 percent since peaking at 10.1 percent, the highest level in twenty-seven years. No one seems to have figured out how to escape the fear that descended following the 2009 bankruptcy of General Motors, an iconic American company if ever there was one; the 2008 collapse of Wall Street investment firms, which supposedly employed America's best and brightest; and the $8 trillion in capital losses arising from the bursting of the real estate bubble.

Life has been especially tough on frontline employees. In a 2009 survey, the Conference Board pegged U.S. job satisfaction at its lowest level in two decades, at 45 percent. That's down from 59 percent in 1995 and 61 percent in 1987.

It's time for a change, and everyone knows it. The very crises that have undermined the priesthood of American business are empowering what was once the underclass: the rebellious, the off kilter, the young, and the marginalized.

This is a book about how businesses have begun to do things differently, and about how you can take advantage of that change. I'll look specifically at how companies have begun to provide more creative freedom to workers, starting with Google's "20 percent time" policy, and then move on to some of the most interesting ways the core ideas behind

20 percent time have flowered and evolved. I'll examine not only 20 percent time per se but also the spirit of 20 percent time—giving people room to tinker and follow their passions, to short-circuit bureaucracy and to innovate independently.

So what is "20 percent time"? It was invented at Google and works like this: Employees at the Internet company are allowed, and sometimes encouraged, to devote a fifth of their time to projects they dreamed up themselves. It could be a day each week, four days each month, or two and a half months each year. There are no hard-and-fast rules; the Googlers and ex-Googlers I've spoken to all made it clear that 20 percent time is above all else an *idea*, a practice that exists more as a widespread understanding than as a written policy.

"Usually, as companies get bigger, they find it really hard to have small, innovative projects," Google cofounder Larry Page said in a 2004 talk. "And we had this problem, too, for a while, and we said, 'Oh, we really need a new concept. . . .' The idea is, for 20 percent of your time, if you're working at Google, you can do what you think is the best thing to do. . . . Many, many useful things come out of this."

The fruits of 20 percent time include the contextual advertising system AdSense, which is Google's second most profitable business line, as well as Gmail; we'll examine those projects more closely later. Twenty percent time also resulted in Google News, Google Reader, the Orkut social network, Google Suggest, and Google Moderator, among others.

Despite these wins, Google's enthusiasm for 20 percent time has waxed and waned. At one point, employees were actively encouraged to pursue 20 percent projects. In recent years, the attitude shifted toward one of mere tolerance. You wouldn't be stopped from diverting your attention to a side project, but your managers could ding you for lack of devotion to officially sanctioned work—no small consideration at a company where bonuses can easily constitute half of an employee's take-home pay. After Page took over as CEO in April 2011, he began tightening the company's focus further, sparking questions in Silicon Valley over whether 20 percent time itself had died. A Google executive has since clarified that 20 percent lives on, but with "a higher bar for what we are going to put to market, sort of an editing function."

Even as it rethinks 20 percent time, Google has done more than any other company to popularize the idea of reserving time for employee creativity. The company evangelized and made high-profile use of an idea that other organizations had previously adopted in more obscure ways. Page devised 20 percent time after he was inspired by flexible work arrangements at Hewlett-Packard and 3M, and by an emphasis on student liberty and spontaneity at Montessori schools, which he and cofounder Sergey Brin attended.

3M was known for its "15 percent time" policy before Google even incorporated. The policy was instituted after a 3M engineer—engineering school dropout, actually, but who's keeping track—defied an order from the company president to stop trying to create a superior "Scotch" masking tape. The engineer by 1925 finished Scotch Masking Tape, which would become one of the company's most iconic products. Because its development was unsanctioned, the tape was often referred to internally as "contraband" tape, and for decades 3M used the term "bootlegging" as shorthand for 15 percent time.

Google's adaptation of 15 percent time is helping the idea of creative independence flower in Silicon Valley and beyond. From National Public Radio to Yahoo, from chef Thomas Keller to the New York City schools, from a New York magazine conglomerate to an Australian business software company, more and more organizations are experimenting with ways to empower individual workers to experiment, hoping to benefit from their innovative ideas in the process.

So-called hack days, where programmers are encouraged to create a software prototype of their choosing within twenty-four hours, began as an attempt to spark 20 percent–style projects on the cheap. They have become wildly popular over the past five years, spreading to Google, Facebook, Twitter, eBay, and other Silicon Valley powerhouses. In a later chapter, I'll show how Yahoo kindled this phenomenon.

In another twist on the original 20 percent concept, some companies invite outsiders to participate in internal side projects, for example, by accepting open-source software patches from independent programmers, by inviting passionate citizens to become "citizen journalists," and by soliciting outside engineers to participate in company coding marathons. The Huffington Post, as you'll see later, used a distributed version of 20 percent time to change how presidential campaigns are covered.

Some of the companies profiled in this book stumbled onto 20 percent–style solutions while trying to create products within their own companies. Others expressly sought to emulate and refine Google's example. For example, Atlassian, a Sydney maker of software tools, has added several features to Google's flavor of 20 percent time. For one, managers are given "get out of work free days" they can use to "steal" employees outside their team to work on a cool idea or side project. Atlassian also imposes some checkpoints on 20 percent time: Any project consuming more than five days must get sign-off from three other "supporters," that is, other developers or managers not directly involved in the project. Any project consuming more than ten days requires sign-off from a founder.

If I sound a little obsessed with side projects and 20 percent–style innovation, that's because I am. In my twelve years as a business journalist, I watched time and time again as companies and technologies that had been relegated to the margins of an industry moved front and center, changing things forever. Covering digital media for Silicon Valley's *Upside* magazine during the dot-com boom, I chronicled how Napster, conceived in a Northeastern University student's dorm room, and Gnutella, written in a few weeks at a renegade division of AOL–Time Warner, revolutionized the distribution of music. Covering high-end restaurants for the *San Francisco Business Times*, I found myself repeatedly writing about how exquisitely trained four-star chefs were making their real fortunes with spin-offs that sold the kind of casual food they typically gave free to their staffs in the back of their high-end kitchens. Writing about technology and media at the gossip blog *Gawker*, I saw firsthand how freewheeling independent bloggers, passionate citizen journalists, and bands of tweeters and Tumblr-ers were thriving while newspapers and broadcast TV networks struggled. Meanwhile, in tech, there seemed to be a sudden explosion of successful companies started on a whim. Mark Zuckerberg famously created

Facebook from his dorm room. Dennis Crowley invented the predecessor to his check-in service Foursquare while working at Jupiter Research and then while a student at NYU. Marco Arment developed the wildly popular iPhone app Instapaper while working as an engineer at Tumblr and trying to figure out a way to read articles during the train ride to work. And so on, and so on.

I didn't just watch the rise of side projects, I was always, in my own small way, trying to participate as well. At *Upside*, I built a meta–search engine that let me query dozens of tech news sites all at once.

At *Gawker*, I built a Web-based comment monitor called Peanuts, named after the proverbial peanut gallery where snarky theater commentators gather. It watched all my recent posts for new reader comments and immediately placed new comments at the top of the page, as well as in alerts on my Mac desktop.

Given my personal enthusiasm for side projects, I could hardly have been more thrilled when a HarperCollins publisher named Debbie Stier approached me with an idea for a book about corporate skunkworks, the small, experimental groups set up within companies but operating with some degree of independence from those companies. Her interest was somewhat personal; at the time she was working in a HarperCollins skunkworks known as Harper Studio.

In the months since, I've completed dozens and dozens of interviews, crashed a pizza-fueled coding spring at craft etailer Etsy's Brooklyn offices, plied sources with wine in Silicon Valley restaurants, and Skyped my face to Australia to interview the grandfather of hackathons.

After surveying an array of companies acting in the spirit of 20 percent time, I decided to home in on some of the more recent and successful among them, with an eye toward assembling a diverse cross section of industries. Each gets its own chapter. Among them, I noticed a set of common tenets, which I'll refer to as the 20 Percent Doctrine:

- **Provide creative freedom.** At their most basic level, systems like 20 percent time are about liberating people from the management structures that dictate their tasks the other 80 percent of the time. They provide mechanisms by which employees can develop ideas normally deemed outside the scope of their job or which are otherwise stifled.

- **Connect with people's passions.** The things people are enthusiastic about and the things they work on every day sometimes diverge, to put it mildly. Twenty percent–style projects are a way to let employees work on projects they find emotionally resonant. Not only is this good for morale, it's good for the resulting projects as well. Customers tend to notice when a product is built with passion by someone who cares.

- **Worse is better.** People developing products in the margins—in the margins of their workweek, in the periphery of their company—must cut some corners if they are ever going to finish anything. Time is tight. Money usually is, too. And in the meantime there are lots of skeptical co-workers and managers to convince. It's imperative to get something out the door. You can always improve upon it later. Version 1 will have to be stripped down, basic, even crude.

- **Embrace reuse.** Almost by definition, 20 percent projects are not about big-bang innovation. The best side projects tend to start as hacks, leveraging some existing product or technology in a clever new way. Reuse lets you launch a project faster and with less work than starting from scratch, crucial advantages for a side project.

- **Iterate quickly.** Just as important as releasing something quickly is improving it quickly. Time and again, successful 20 percent–style projects have used iteration to snowball their way to success within the host company. Releasing a stream of improvements creates a positive feedback loop: Each improvement generates discussion, draws attention, and encourages supporters.

- **Communicate lessons as you learn them.** The unspoken agenda of every 20 percent–style project is to become a full-blown company initiative. The creators of successful side projects are, thus, always selling. They are selling to their bosses, from whom they'd like resources; they are selling to other employees, from whom they'd like help; and they are selling to their existing helpers, whom they'd like to keep around. So it's no accident that they find ways to regularly share lessons they've learned and their ideas for moving forward.

- **Embrace outsiders.** Side projects tend to be especially allergic to insular thinking and especially receptive to outside ideas. Selling and realizing a disruptive vision is not an easy thing to do, especially when the people you're selling to are the ones you're trying to disrupt. Outsiders can help. Twenty percent–style projects tend to reach outside the usual channels for help. Sometimes that means working with someone in a different company group, and sometimes it means turning to people outside the company. Help can come in the form of actual work, advice, publicity, or public affirmation.

My exploration of the 20 Percent Doctrine in the coming chapters is designed for smart people on the front lines of business. Whether you're an individual worker trying to inject innovation into your company or a manager trying to bubble a new idea upward, the principles outlined above can help you create a "virtual start-up," to borrow a phrase from tech entrepreneur Anil Dash, without quitting your job. Launching such a project requires hacking the corporate org chart, cutting through red tape, and drawing support across internal lines of authority. The 20 Percent Doctrine can help. I'm not saying it will be easy. You'll need a lot of chutzpah, a fine-tuned sense of your own political position within the company, the ability to create things outside the usual channels, some genuinely good ideas, and at least a little bit of luck. But knowing what helped others who came before will at least give you a fighting chance.

As we examine the flowering of 20 percent–style projects, you'll learn to personally catalyze innovation rather than watching in frustration as change overtakes your organization. Rebelliousness plays a starring role. You'll meet engineer Paul Buchheit, who created a $10 billion-per-year revenue stream for Google because he was smart enough to ignore the boss who told him to stop working on it. You'll meet Joan Sullivan, who built a top-ranked public high school in the nation's poorest congressional district by bypassing old rules on hiring teachers, ignoring old models of how public schools should be funded, and demolishing old expectations for students. And you'll meet Chad Dickerson, who went rogue within Yahoo to create the Woodstock of hackathons.

You'll also see examples of creating successful 20 percent–style projects with limited time and resources. When acclaimed chef Thomas Keller had to build a restaurant at breakneck speed, he ended up making one of the most beloved and novel restaurants going today. Similarly, without a cash crisis, the pioneering website Flickr would not have emerged to introduce photo sharing to the world.

In addition, you'll see how creative use of online communication tools multiplies the effectiveness of side projects, including Huffington Post's Off the Bus citizen journalism initiative, which redefined a presidential campaign by coordinating a large army of volunteer journalists and carefully sifting the information they provided.

There's never been a better time to hatch a 20 percent–style project. It's become cheaper and easier to get new ventures going, thanks to computing advances, accelerating Internet speeds, and the globalization of manufacturing. Meanwhile, start-up culture is very much in vogue again with the resurgence of the tech industry. The 20 Percent Doctrine offers ways to bring the spirit of a start-up to your company and to co-opt corporate resources without the risks of striking out on your own.

For all the rational reasons to explore the 20 Percent Doctrine, the most important catalyst for exploring these ideas is probably emotional. Creating things freely and directly just feels good. As tech publisher Dale Dougherty recently said, "All of us are makers—we're born makers. . . . We don't just live but we *make*, we create things." What follows is a guide to exercising your natural urge to make in a way that's compatible with the complexities of modern life—and with your current job.

Scratching Your Own Itch

Paul Buchheit's Dark Struggle to Launch Gmail

At 3 A.M. one day in Mountain View, California, a software engineer named Paul Buchheit made a promise to his manager, Google vice president Marissa Mayer, with whom he had been working late at company headquarters. He pledged not to press forward with his idea for "creepy and weird" text ads based on the contents of one's e-mail in-box. "I remember leaving," Mayer later said, "and when I walked out the door I stopped for a minute, and I remember I leaned back and I said, 'So, Paul, we agreed we're not exploring the whole ad thing right now, right?' And he was like, 'Yup, right.'"

Buchheit broke his word almost immediately. Over the next few hours, he hacked together a prototype of "the ad thing," a system that would read your e-mail and automatically find a related ad to display next to it. The advertising system would fund Gmail, an advanced new e-mail system he had invented. When, the next morning, his coworkers saw what he had created, they called it blasphemy. Mayer thought about ordering Buchheit, asleep at home, to drag himself out of bed and pull the plug on his creation.

Luckily, she didn't. "This story is a lot of egg on my face," Mayer later said in a Stanford University podcast. Buchheit's system, called AdSense, makes Google around $10 billion in revenue each year. You've probably seen AdSense's trademark blue-and-white ads in page margins all over the Web.

Through his long struggle to launch AdSense and its companion product, Gmail, which boasts hundreds of millions of users, Buchheit transformed Google from a company narrowly focused on search to one with a bigger vision of itself, a company expanding quickly into new markets by following the passions of its employees. The mild-mannered engineer proved to Google high command the value of letting frontline programmers push the company into new markets.

"I think I may have something to do with 20 percent projects," Buchheit told start-up adviser Jessica Livingston, "because I've created a few things on the side. . . . Inevitably . . . something catches my eye and I go off and work on it for a little bit." In other words, before Google proved the value of 20 percent time to the world, Paul Buchheit proved it to Google.

He did so by embracing an idea that should be at the core of any 20 percent–style project: Before you can create a product that solves problems for other people, you must be able to create a product that solves problems for you. Gmail and AdSense addressed issues that, first and foremost, bothered Paul Buchheit. Slowly but surely they grew to address the needs of Buchheit's immediate coworkers. Then Buchheit set a goal of making one hundred Googlers happy with his creations. Only later were they released to the public. By putting himself at the center of his development process, Buchheit created products beloved by millions of users, to say nothing of Google's shareholders.

If you're trying to launch your own side project, the takeaway from Gmail and AdSense is that before you can sell the project to your boss you first to need to make something you yourself would buy into. Scratching your own itch provides the motivation to work on something above and beyond your regular duties. Everything Buchheit did was possible because he built first and foremost for himself. The emotional payoff to what he was doing helped Buchheit push past many obstacles.

The process of turning your personal wants into products that help others is remakably visceral.

"Just notice problems that are around you," Buchheit told a gathering of aspiring entrepreneurs in 2008. "Kind of stop and pay attention to what's going on inside your own body, your own mind. . . . Start to notice every time you have to wait for something or every time you get slightly confused or aggravated with the product, every small annoyance . . . most of the things we put into Gmail were just, like, I was annoyed with something, and we would try to think of a solution for it."

The process of turning annoyances into products is also deeply satisfying. "The more you feel that you can control your environment, and that the things you do are actually working, the happier you are," software guru Joel Spolsky has written, citing research into "learned helplessness" by the renowned psychologist Martin Seligman. "When you find yourself frustrated, angry, and upset, it's probably because of something that happened that you could not control: even something small. The space bar on your keyboard is not working well. . . . The key to your front door doesn't work very well. . . . These things add up."

The story of Gmail and AdSense began in August 2001, when Buchheit finished work on Google Groups, an archive of online conversations from an old part of the Internet known as "Usenet." Buchheit's job was to make the archive searchable. He did a very good job: Buchheit's system let users find posts within particular message boards, called "newsgroups"; messages written by particular people; and messages within a certain range of dates. It was eventually recognized with a "product excellence" award from the well-regarded programming magazine *Dr. Dobb's Journal*. Internally, Google Groups just earned Buchheit more work: a mandate to build some sort of search personalization product. Google's mission was to organize and make useful all of the world's information, but much of that knowledge was locked away within people's private troves. The particulars of solving that problem were left up to Buchheit.

"I was given a kind of vague direction to work on some kind of e-mail or related project," Buchheit told me.

The engineer knew what he wanted to do. Ever since he was a student at Case Western Reserve University in the 1990s, Buchheit had wanted to put e-mail on the Web. Back then, checking e-mail meant firing up crude specialized software. Buchheit, ever the tinkerer, began building a website that could bring up his e-mail from any Web browser anywhere. He eventually abandoned the project, busy with other things.

E-mail was still bugging Buchheit after he got to Google, which had the most advanced e-mail software available. The engineer was swamped with five hundred messages per day, many from Googlers talking past one another in the same conversation, their in-boxes so cluttered they missed one another's messages. People came up with awkward coping strategies, like religiously sorting their conversations into folders, or ruthlessly deleting old messages, losing valuable history in the process. Buchheit himself found it nearly impossible to navigate his in-box. "It was all really confusing for me," he later said.

It took just a few hours for Buchheit to create a prototype of what he dubbed "Gmail," thanks to an ingenious shortcut: Buchheit simply took the code he had written to search Google Groups and set it loose on his personal e-mail archive. It helped that e-mail messages are nearly identical to Usenet messages. Both have fields like "To:," "From:," "Date:," and "Subject:," and follow the same formatting rules (a historic document called RFC 822). As we'll see later, this type of reuse is a common pattern among successful 20 percent projects.

The first Gmail was pretty darn basic. Buchheit had not had time to code support for more than one account. Yet the programmer didn't let the rudimentary state of Gmail keep him from showing it off to colleagues, to whom he e-mailed a link to the service. "They said that it was somewhat useful," he later deadpanned on his blog, "but it would be better if it searched over their e-mail instead of mine."

As requested, Gmail 2.0 let people search their own mail. By version three, users could even reply to messages, a feature requested by Google cofounders Larry Page and Sergey Brin, two of Gmail's first users. Buchheit later added "conversation view," which displayed all replies to an e-mail message as a unified thread on a single Web page, hiding copies of prior e-mails appended to the bottom of subsequent messages. At last, Buchheit had come up with a way to keep his coworkers from talking past one another. They'd have to read all prior replies to an e-mail *before* they could send one of their own.

Like Gmail's search feature, conversation view was built quickly using code Buchheit adapted from Google Groups. Buchheit kept launching new prototypes, one after another in rapid succession, all internal to Google. He was practicing an increasingly popular software development technique: Release early and iterate often, with a slew of new versions. The churn of the early Gmail code base was intense, so intense that the front end was rewritten about six times and the back end three times before the product was ever shown to the public.

As he refined Gmail, Buchheit was methodically eliminating his own workday annoyances and those of his colleagues at Google. "Every time we would get irritated by some little problem," he told Livingston, "or one of the [internal Google] users would, we'd just spend time thinking about it, looking at what the underlying problems are and how we can come up with solutions."

Buchheit said that this sort of rapid improvement was the key to the success of Gmail. Iteration is how Buchheit took a website designed by and for himself and turned it into something that was useful to other people. It allowed Buchheit to show people he was incorporating their ideas, to get feedback on flaws not apparent to him, and to generate discussion on how to grow the product. Brin and Page became crucial early champions of Gmail, thanks to their participation in this feedback loop.

Buchheit later called Gmail's development process "the humble approach to product design."

"What's the right attitude? Humility," he wrote on his blog. "It doesn't matter how smart and successful and qualified you are, you simply don't know what you're doing. The good news is that nobody else does, either, though some are foolish enough to think that they do (and that's why you can beat them). . . .

"Pay attention. Notice which things are working and which aren't. Experiment and iterate. Question your assumptions. Remember that you are wrong about a lot of things. Watch for the signals. Lose your technical and design snobbery. Whatever works, works . . . you should consider spending less time talking, and more time prototyping."

Anyone embarking on a 20 percent time project can benefit from the sort of iterative feedback loop Buchheit established when developing Gmail. The trick is to find a way to make a small initial prototype and then to take small steps forward. If you're too ambitious and the steps are too large, the iterations take longer and your feedback loop loses energy—fewer coworkers talking about your project or sending in suggestions, fewer new versions to try, and less internal mindshare for your experiment. The best way to keep your steps small is to keep your very first prototype small. In the world of tech start-ups, this minification is referred to as creating the "Minimum Viable Product." While your ego, fears, and superiors tend to push you toward a bigger, more impressive first release, the religion of Minimum Viable Product preaches the virtues of starting small. The sooner you release, the sooner you get information from your users about where the product should go. It might feel embarrassing to release something as crude as Gmail 1.0. But embarrassing yourself in front of your first customers is better than never interacting with them in the first place.

It can be hard to know when you're done iterating—when a 20 percent time project has gestated long enough and can be considered both conceptually proven and sufficiently developed. Buchheit, on the advice of then-CEO Eric Schmidt, decided "we should get 100 happy users inside of Google before launching." This proved tricky. "I was like, 'Oh, that's easy, Google has like thousands of employees,'" he said at the 2008 gathering of aspiring entrepreneurs. "But it turns out happiness is a really high bar, and to get people to say that they're happy was actually sort of challenging."

"We literally did it one user at a time. We would go to people and be like, 'Okay, what's it going to take to make you happy?' And in some cases, they would ask for something really hard, and we'd be like, 'Okay, well, you're not going to be happy with Gmail, quite possibly ever.' But with other people it turned out there would be something really small we could do and then they'd be happy. And so we'd do the really easy things until we finally got 100 people who were happy. And 100 doesn't sound like a lot but it turns out people are pretty similar to each other, so if you can make 100 people happy, usually you can make more [happy]."

Buchheit and the team he later assembled used iteration

to steadily overcome opposition within Google. After all, the surest way to shatter a preconception is with direct evidence to the contrary, and each new version of Gmail did a better job than the last, proving Google could do something awesome and transformative for e-mail. Each one of Buchheit's improvements converted more skeptics into allies.

And there were plenty of skeptics. Former Googler Chris Wetherell, who helped create Google Reader, remembers being amazed at the team's ability to pull through.

"Can you imagine working on it for two years?" he asked me. "No daylight. Very little feedback. Many [interface] iterations, many. Some so bad that people thought, 'This will never launch, this is the worst thing ever.' I remember being in a meeting, and a founding member [of Google], I don't want to say which one, said, 'This is brand destroying. This will destroy our brand. This will crush our company.'" (Buchheit has said Gmail development was tough, but didn't remember sentiment being so extreme when I asked him about this quote.)

It's hard to imagine today, when Gmail has hundreds of millions of users, and when Google makes everything from a smartphone operating system to office software to a blog platform, but for years many Googlers opposed on principle the idea of venturing beyond search, believing the company should add only niche products like news search, shopping search, Usenet search like Google Groups, and so on. Gmail took the company way beyond that. "People weren't sure we should even be doing this," Buchheit told Livingston. "So the general attitude would swing, and when it would swing against us, that was very hard to deal with."

He later wrote, "For a long time, almost everyone disliked

it. . . . Quite a few people thought that we should kill the project."

Buchheit overcame the objections by showing how much better an e-mail system could be when it had strong search capabilities. It's no accident that search was Gmail's first feature; other e-mail programs just sucked at it. They were typically very slow at running queries and in many cases could not search the body of an e-mail, only the subject line and other headers. Gmail, in contrast, searched as fast and comprehensively as Google.com.

And it kept getting better. Initially, Gmail didn't include your newest e-mails since, like Google.com, it incorporated new data only every half hour or so. That was fine for finding Web pages, but too slow for e-mail, and Buchheit iterated until it was fixed.

Google's Gmail haters also took aim at Gmail's heavy use of JavaScript, the programming language built into all Web browsers. When Gmail was under development, JavaScript was primarily known for powering annoying pop-up advertisements and juvenile animations, and detractors thought Buchheit was investing way too heavily in it. Some even advocated rewriting Gmail as native software that ran directly on your PC.

But as Buchheit played with JavaScript, he grew more impressed. He had begun tinkering with the language to fulfill a feature request from one of those first hundred users he was trying to delight. There was no way to implement the feature using a conventional HTML Web page, so Buchheit added some JavaScript. That worked so well, he began turning to JavaScript for other features. The language eventually made Gmail feel like a desktop e-mail program like Microsoft Outlook, as opposed to a clunky series of Web pages like Hotmail.com. For example, writing a message on Hotmail could easily require four page loads: one for "new message," one to open your address book, one to search it, and one to pick a recipient. On Gmail, you clicked just once, and JavaScript generated the blank message form right away. If you started to type your friend's name, Gmail would offer to autocomplete his e-mail address. This felt like magic. But it came together through a series of simple iterations that Buchheit could deploy one at a time—the instant "new message" button, recipient autocomplete, and finally the ability to send an e-mail without leaving the page. Each step further proved the viability of JavaScript.

The pushback over Google expansion and JavaScript were mere preludes to the abuse Buchheit would take over the contextual advertising system he invented, AdSense. Buchheit created AdSense to pay for the spiraling costs of Gmail. Gmail was expensive to operate because it allowed users to store a full gigabyte of e-mails, roughly five hundred times as many as competitors Hotmail and Yahoo! Mail. Mayer, Gmail's product manager, an early employee, and an influential VP, wanted Buchheit to follow the traditional path to finance this—charging users for extra storage. But Buchheit's mind turned instead to contextual advertisements of the sort Google served up alongside its search results. They were, after all, making the company a fortune.

The advertising system, AdWords, worked like this: If you searched for, say, "Paris vacation," Google would show you an ad for, say, a Paris hotel, since the hotel selected those

keywords for its ads, knowing that many of its tourist customers ran searches using them. What if, Buchheit wondered,
Google could infer your intentions—visiting Paris—from
your e-mail, without you having to type anything into a
search box? Instead of selecting ads based on keywords you
typed into Google.com, AdSense would select ads based on
keywords distilled from your Gmail message, or indeed from
any Web page.

It was a technically brilliant idea, but it also sounded creepy
as hell when you described it in simple terms: *Google reads your
e-mail to target ads at you.* "At first, it kind of seems a little bit
wrong, right?" Buchheit told Livingston. "Everyone hated
it. . . . Someone may have used the word 'blasphemous.' "

Mayer was ready to kill AdSense. Gmail wasn't yet done.
It didn't even send e-mail reliably. And in any case she wanted
to stick with the idea of charging for larger mailboxes like
Hotmail and Yahoo! Mail did.

"I was like, 'Paul, Paul, Paul—ads are never going to
work,' " Mayer said on the Stanford podcast. "I was like, 'Because, you know, either we're going to run banner ads and
they're not going to be targeted and people develop blind
spots that are horrible in terms of effectiveness, and we'll
never make any money, *or* we're going to target the ads at their
e-mail, which is just going to be creepy and weird. People are
going to think there are people here reading their e-mails and
picking out the ads and it's going to be terrible.' "

"We're not going to worry about money," she told him
on her way out of the office at 3 A.M. "Let's work on actually,
like, sending, receiving, and reading email."

Luckily for Buchheit, empirical results trump

preconceptions in Google's culture. Just as he had overcome some of the skepticism about Gmail by developing a bare-bones prototype to show people, Buchheit would demolish the idea that AdSense was "creepy" by putting it in front of the critics. So even after Mayer made him promise not to build a prototype, he built one anyway, gambling that it would prove Mayer wrong.

After Mayer was safely out of the building, Buchheit worked quickly. Mayer would be back soon for the next day's work, after all. In what remained of the night, Buchheit wanted not only to create an AdSense prototype, but to demolish a long-held Google truism that automatically targeting ads to content was basically unworkable, requiring esoteric computer science like artificial intelligence.

Buchheit's approach was, once again, to build the simplest thing that could possibly work. Illuminated by the glow of his monitor, Buchheit retrieved into his code editor a software filter he'd created to screen for adult content. Normally, the filter examined a batch of known porn pages and listed words that occurred disproportionately within those pages. Other pages containing those words were then assumed to be porn. Buchheit instead turned the filter on Gmail messages, using the resulting keywords to select advertisements from Google's AdWords database. Buchheit, in other words, adapted the porn filter for AdSense just as he adapted his Usenet searcher for e-mail.

After several rounds of editing and debugging, Buchheit's adaptation worked. He released AdSense to Gmail's all-Googler user base before finally getting up from his chair. It was 7 A.M. by the time he stumbled out of the office in a sleepy daze, Mayer later said (Buchheit doesn't remember staying quite so late).

Mayer discovered AdSense a few hours after Buchheit created it, when she came back into the office for the start of the next workday. Panicked to suddenly see his "creepy" ads inserted into the margins of her Gmail messages, Mayer thought about calling the engineer to demand they be removed. But Buchheit had been working all night, according to Google's internal logs, and was probably just getting to bed at home. As much as she feared that Page and Brin might see AdSense and love it—they had "weird views about privacy, and what's creepy and what's not," Mayer later said—she thought it was more important to give Buchheit the mercy of a couple of hours of sleep.

While she waited, Mayer checked her Gmail. There was an e-mail from a friend who invited her to go hiking—and next to it, an ad for hiking boots. Another e-mail was about Al Gore coming to speak at Stanford University—and next to it was an ad for books about Al Gore. Just a couple of hours after the system had been invented, Mayer grudgingly admitted to herself, AdSense was already useful, entertaining, and relevant. Of course, not everyone at Google was a fan. "I don't remember there being a lot of positive feedback when I showed up for work," Buchheit told me. "Random people in the hallways would mention not liking [the ads]."

The right people seemed to like them, though. Like Mayer, Page and Brin loved AdSense. In short order, the Google high command decided AdSense would be a top priority. It was a no-brainer: Google's main revenue source, AdWords, placed contextual ads alongside search results. But search results were just 5 percent of Web views; AdSense promised to open up the other 95 percent to ads, since it could go inside *any* Web page.

"There's no question that Larry and Sergey realized the potential and quickly spun up a project to turn it into a real product," Buchheit told me. "Without their fearless openness to new ideas and projects, a lot of great things never would have happened."

Even if you don't have your company's founders beta testing your product, as Buchheit did, you can still learn from his willingness to defy and his readiness to adapt.

By ignoring Mayer's direct instruction from 3 A.M. until roughly 7 A.M. one morning, Buchheit showed that a little rebellion can go a long way. He didn't quite put his job on the line. If things had gone pear shaped, he could have always claimed sleep deprivation. And he'd earned a little latitude, given the late hours he was putting in. If you think you've earned a little leeway, too, keep an eye out for opportunities to be strategically rebellious.

You should also try following Buchheit's lead in adapting old work. For Gmail, Buchheit reused his Usenet search engine. For AdSense, he adapted a porn filter. Because he wasn't building from scratch, Buchheit avoided bugs and accelerated development. "A lot of times people think that hard problems demand complex solutions," Buchheit told engineer Kaustubh Katdare, "but we've found that the opposite is often the case."

This sort of adaptation is a pattern we'll see over and over again, not just in software but in food, politics, and anywhere else people are trying to simplify the creation of products addressing complicated problems. As tempting as it is to start with a clean slate, always look for opportunities to use something old to create something fresh. In the collaborative tech industry, people who haven't mastered the skill of adaptive reuse are said to have contracted "Not Invented Here" syndrome, which prevents them from seeing or appreciating innovation from other people or companies. Having Not Invented Here syndrome means you waste time reinventing the wheel. When you're working in 20 percent time, with little time to burn, having NIH is especially harmful.

Buchheit continued to refine AdSense and gave it time to sink in with other Googlers. It did; soon other staff members were praising the system.

It took just six months to launch AdSense to the public. The ad platform debuted in June 2003 as a stand-alone product, an advertising widget that any publisher—from a lone blogger to a giant media company—could attach to any Web page. It generates around $10 billion per year, making it Google's second-biggest source of revenue after AdWords. AdSense's original reason for being, Gmail, launched on April 1, 2004, after a total of two and a half years of development. (Because of the date, some people thought the product, and its extraordinary 1 GB of e-mail storage, was part of an elaborate hoax.) Gmail became the fastest-growing Web mail service, and now claims upwards of 200 million users. All because one determined engineer wanted to solve a problem he was having around the office.

Buchheit's experience contains lessons for how to build a 20 percent time project—scratch your own itch, rebel a little if need be, make a prototype quickly to prove your idea, and iterate improvements quickly.

But there are also lessons in how to sell, nurture, and protect a 20 percent time project in the ways Buchheit adapted to his company environment.

As anyone who has done a side project can attest, it is extraordinary that Buchheit finagled enough resources from Google to sustain Gmail for two and a half years before it launched to the public, particularly at a time before the company had established its 20 percent culture.

Buchheit was fortunate to have powerful users of his products and smart enough to take advantage of this. He had a friendship with Mayer, employee number 20 and a heavy hitter at Google. Cofounders Page and Brin were early and enthusiastic testers of Gmail. These connections gave Buchheit the room to defiantly create his AdSense prototype and laid the fertile soil in which this defiance could be embraced and made productive. AdSense, in turn, was the financial engine that made Gmail possible. Having powerful friends was no doubt also helpful to Buchheit when he was under fire from Google purists who didn't want the company to expand beyond search, or when Buchheit needed more staff or hard drives for Gmail.

Wetherell has a cautionary tale of what can happen at Google when your 20 percent project doesn't have the sponsors and high-level support Gmail got. His project, Google Reader, evolved into the market's preeminent aggregator of RSS feeds, which deliver news items in an open format. But it became something of a black sheep inside Google, deprived of resources and denied opportunities to integrate with other products.

Google Reader greatly accelerates the process of surfing the Web. Using the Google Reader website, you can keep up to date with your favorite blogs and websites, seeing at a glance which ones have new updates. You can also organize clusters of sites into folders and view items from those sites mixed together, sorted by recency. Wetherell began building it after he realized how easy it would be to repurpose software he had written to parse news feeds inside a Web browser. His vision was to let people aggregate feeds right in the browser and to apply tags to them.

Wetherell, who was assigned to Google's Blogger product, asked for a little time off to develop his idea and, thanks to 20 percent time, got it. Wetherell told me, "It was easy to go to people and have conversations and say, 'Can I just run with this for a second if there's no large objections?' And it was easy for them to say, 'Here's where we feel comfortable: You need to take that day, go for it.' They felt covered. If someone asked them, they could justify it—'that guy's doing something 20 percent on that Friday.'"

Wetherell had his bosses on board. He was even able to sidestep the "gauntlet" review process that Google had by then established for new products. Google Reader initially billed itself as being a "dependency," or subproduct, of a customizable home page called iGoogle, which already had approval. Plus, Google Reader managed to rope in two longtime employees who could place software on Google's servers without going through the normal chain of command.

These tactics are worth considering if you're trying to get

a side project off the ground quickly: Try snatching resources under the aegis of a more established project and leverage access to system administrators and computer systems. Buch-heit used similar subterfuge to launch AdSense, working on the contextual advertising when he was supposed to be working on Gmail proper, and launching it using his special access to the databases powering Google's original advertising system, AdWords.

But flying under the radar had a big downside in Google Reader's case, which was that the project never found a spon-sor among Google's top executives. "We kept running into the problem where, if you're 20 percent and you got to launch, people who actually have the decision-making power did not create this thing, so they're constantly in a position of needing to be convinced of its value," Wetherell told me. "They are saying, 'Well, I just found out about two new things. There is this video site called YouTube that seems to be very [popu-lar], and I need to grab some resources for that. . . . Why am I caring about your thing?'

"People were using [Google Reader] every day. They woke up with it. They couldn't live without it. This was a lot of people. But it's not the same amount of people as searching. It's not the same amount of people as using Google Maps."

Impatient with Google Reader, Google's high command eventually forced a premature birth, ordering the Google Reader team to ship it in time for the 2005 Web 2.0 confer-ence, just one month away. At that point, Google Reader had been under development for only around six months, and did not even allow the user to subscribe to feeds, among the most basic functionality a feed reader can have. Google Reader improved greatly in its subsequent versions, but it never shed the stigma from its rushed launch.

"There is no question that that hurt us long term, mostly in terms of where it positioned us in the company, forever. Forever. As this niche thing—'[we're] not involved, [we] can't tie this rather strong product to your weak product'— forever. That was a hell of a decision and a huge lesson for me personally . . . that if you're the core contributor of a project, or one of the core contributors in a product and if you don't control the ship date, you may have a problem."

Another thing Buchheit did well was to embrace the chaos that surrounded him at Google, a company that welcomed the disorder that naturally occurs in fast-moving companies, within fast-changing markets, and among driven, creative workers. Indeed, a "brink of chaos management model" is how Google's system was described in a collection of Harvard Business School case studies by management guru Gary Hamel, and that's an apt description for a company that's structured in many ways like the Internet itself: a place of frank feedback, rapidly churning ideas, and flattened hierarchies. Internal meetings are freewheeling, with Googlers loudly sharing their opinions with little regard for status and lines of authority. Everyone has a right to be taken seriously. The innovation process can be brutally Darwinist; VP Mayer has estimated that as many as 80 percent of the experiments ultimately fail.

Buchheit turned this unsparing environment to his advantage. Rather than chafe when his passion project was called "brand destroying" and "the worst thing ever," as Wetherell recalled it, he immersed himself in the feedback, setting a goal of making one hundred users happy with the product. Anyone trying to nurture a side project should try to accept even the most withering feedback in a similarly humble and constructive manner. Doing so goes hand in hand with the 20 Percent Doctrine principles of iterating quickly and communicating lessons. If you're not listening closely to the people evaluating your product, it's going to be much harder to improve said product.

Of course, Buchheit did more than just listen to suggestions and frank feedback from his users. He also tested solutions to their problems. Google has made something of a religion out of testing, measurement, and statistical analysis. Even top Google executives must abide by the requirement to back their ideas up with data. To help prove the value of one idea they supported, a massive digital archive of books, Mayer and Page went so far as to clamp a three-hundred-page book to a piece of plywood, manually photograph each of its pages, and run the images through character recognition software, all to establish that it would only take forty minutes to digitize a book.

Buchheit did plenty of testing with Gmail, as well. Indeed, a key feature of his iterative approach was that it provided many opportunities to try things on his test users and to collect data about the results. "A lot of features seemed like great ideas, until we tried them," he later blogged. "Other things seemed like they would be big problems or very confusing, but once they were in, we forgot all about the theoretical problems. The great thing about this process was that I didn't need to sell anyone on my ideas. I would just write the code, release the feature, and watch the response. Usually, everyone (including me) would end up hating whatever it was (especially my ideas), but we always learned something from the experience, and we were able to quickly move on to other ideas."

Testing should become your obsession if you're trying to build up support for a side project. Iterative testing will help you both improve your product and make a business case for it. As with Mayer's book-scanning experiment, the right sort of test can help establish how much time and money a project will need in order to move forward and whether it is technically viable. With that information in hand, you can construct a believable scenario for how your product will turn a profit.

Another thing Buchheit did was to manage horizontally rather than just up the chain of command. In other words, he effectively reached out to his peers for ideas, feedback, and support, and he recruited some of them to his cause. This sort of outreach is important for any 20 percent–style project, but it's especially crucial at Google, where the management hierarchy is very flat and employees have a lot of freedom to move around from project to project. At Google, employees have been organized into small teams; when Hamel studied the company, the teams averaged three engineers each, though they have reportedly grown since then to roughly six. Employees work with few layers of managers above them; the average product development manager had more than fifty direct reports, according to Hamel, while some managers had more than one hundred. The management structure is said to have become at least somewhat more vertical in recent years.

In some ways, Google resembles a university graduate school. As at a university, most people are doing multiple things at once. A typical Google engineer is on multiple teams and is encouraged to switch to projects she is interested in committing to rather than being assigned to one. Work schedules can be very fluid; the "20 percent time" system means people can take a day a week to work on whatever they want, but it also means they can work for ten months on a core company product and then two months on whatever they want, not unlike a student on summer break. And Google has historically made no real effort to police what an employee might do in such a period of experimentation.

Google helps encourage peer-to-peer communication with a variety of online systems. At the individual level, this can be as simple as trading e-mail—a huge part of Google's culture—or instant messages. More specialized systems include, at the individual level, a "Snippets" site, where engineers post weekly updates, sharing their activity. At the project level, Google offers on its intranet a system called MOMA, which gives every project in the company (several hundred) its own threaded conversation. At the group level, there's the Misc List, a freewheeling forum attached to each Google team and used for comments and ideas. At the company level, there's a weekly event called "TGIF" at a café in the Googleplex, where cofounders Larry Page and Sergey Brin talk about milestones and new hires and take questions.

Not all of these systems existed when Buchheit began his work on Gmail. Nevertheless, the engineer did a good job of reaching out to his peers. In part, this was out of necessity; due to its generous one-gigabyte storage quota, Gmail was ravenous for hard drives, and Buchheit scrounged around for them from various corners of the organization, including by begging his colleagues in other groups for their disused drives. A few months into Gmail's development, Buchheit added fellow Google engineers Sanjeev Singh and Jing Lim to his team. He worked his way up to about a dozen staff by the time Gmail launched.

One reason Gmail would have been attractive to Google's world-class programmers is that it was initially so bad. Engineers, keep in mind, like to fix things. And like other creative professionals, they like to show off their skills. Wetherell used this to his advantage in Google Reader's early days, when he was trying to put together a team.

"I reached very quickly the limit of my engineering capability," he told me. "Even though I worked at Google as a Senior Software Engineer, I'm not as good as the other engineers there. . . . I showed my initial attempts to do this to an engineer, a guy named Mihai Parparita. I said, 'I think there's a whole bunch of things here and I've a few ideas and I've done a pretty good job.' And I thought that, no, I hadn't. He looked at [the code] and I thought he was going to run from the room. He just saw this wounded code and he said, 'It's going to have to be a lot better than that.' But that inspired him, like he was all 'Oh' and he also then took more of his time."

Whether it was Buchheit begging for hard drives or Wetherell asking advice about his attempt to write a flexible software framework for Google Reader, showing weakness and need is often a better way to attract help from your peers than hiding your vulnerabilities. A struggling 20 percent–style project can take inspiration from the folktale about stone soup. In that story, hungry travelers are unable to beg any food after arriving at a village, so they fill their pot with water and a stone, stoking the villagers' curiosity. "What are you making?" one asks. "Stone soup," comes the reply. "It's wonderful, but it could use some garnish." The villager contributes a bit of carrot. Another villager comes along and asks the same question, getting the same answer. He donates some scraps of meat. The process of curiosity and sharing repeats with other villagers, who contribute seasoning, vegetables, and so on. Eventually, stone soup is transformed into the real thing.

Similarly, a side project slowly becomes a real project by a process of accumulation. A scrap of help here, a scrap of help there. When you're building a product this way, you want to project the same combination of confidence and need as the stone soup chef, or as Buchheit or Wetherell. On the one hand, sell your vision and the awesomeness of whatever you're working on. On the other hand, don't hide the fact that you need some help. Your best potential allies won't be scared off by that; they'll be excited.

2

20 Percent on the Cheap

How Flickr's Constraints Made It a Fortune

Today, there's no doubt Flickr is a brilliant product; the world's first big photo website, it is home to more than 6 billion pictures and made a reported $30 million for its creators. But Flickr was almost shot down before it could take off. "The vote was actually tied," said Caterina Fake, remembering the referendum she and partner Stewart Butterfield called to determine whether their broke start-up should build what became Flickr. "There were six of us voting, but Stewart and I guilted Eric Costello into voting with us, so we got him to switch sides. . . . There was one guy who didn't like the Flickr idea and had voted against it, so he went to work on another [company] similar to classmates.com."

The divisive Flickr vote is just one illustration of how much more contentious it can be to launch a 20 percent–style project at a start-up: Resources are constrained; there is no capital, staff, or time to spare; and there is no margin for wrong turns. By consuming precious attention, Flickr represented both hope and a potentially lethal challenge to the Canadian video game company where it was born.

But tight resources ended up being precisely what made Flickr successful. An almost desperate hunger to win and win quickly, to accumulate users and revenue, motivated the Flickr team to listen closely to their users. A lack of money and a lack of other advantages opened them to the ad hoc and unconventional. In the end, it was the founders' *needs* that led them to remake their company around Flickr—their need for revenue, their need for focus, and their need to take risks. The masterful way they turned desperation into a new beginning has since been given a name, "pivoting," and it has been embraced widely among Silicon Valley start-ups, including by the people who built the booming microblogging service Twitter.

Anyone launching a 20 percent–style project with few resources would be well advised to study Flickr, and in particular its exploitation of its own constraints. And what 20 percent project *isn't* resource-constrained? Rare is the lavishly funded side project; getting lots money tends to disqualify you from calling a something a "side project" in the first place. But you can turn poverty to your advantage. Flickr is a case study in how powerful a motivator it can be to be short on time and money. Most of the things that made Gmail successful—a stripped-down prototype, fast iteration, and defiant bravery—are catalyzed by the hunger you get in a tight environment. Flickr made impossible deadlines and an empty bank account its friends, and you can, too.

Flickr was born as a last resort. "We were out of money," Fake told me.

She had begun her start-up a year and a half prior, with husband Stewart Butterfield and their programmer friend Jason Classon. Fake and Butterfield's honeymoon had just ended, and a sense of revelry suffused their new venture, which they dubbed "Ludicorp," after *ludus*, the Latin word for "play."

Ludicorp's sole product, a social Web adventure called Game Neverending, was inspired by the Internet games Fake and Butterfield had played as research for a kids' website Butterfield built for the Canadian Broadcasting Corporation. It had a quirky style; rather than blasting enemies, slaying dragons, or piloting a spaceship, as in other games, players interacted socially. They could forge alliances, leave messages, and invent new objects. The game was set in an imaginary, graphical world, a world not unlike the one in NeoPets, an animal care game Fake had grown addicted to. Game Neverending also had social features, which were inspired by an old text-based adventure environment called LamdaMOO. The social element of Game Neverending capitalized on Fake's experience running online communities for Netscape and for the early online magazine *Electric Minds*.

Game Neverending was supposed to be "lightweight," as Fake put it, a forerunner to the sort of casual games people now play on Facebook. Ludicorp was, likewise, a lean affair. The company launched in 2002, after the dot-com boom had turned into a severe recession. Investors were hard to come by, so Fake and Butterfield seeded their venture with money from friends and family, and with the proceeds from a company Butterfield and Classon had sold a few years earlier. In the interest of thrift, Ludicorp tried to exploit the economic downturn, starting with the battered market for office space; it saved money by subletting a sublet, the sort of arrangement no landlord would have accepted two years earlier. The company also hired conservatively, peaking at seven employees in its thirty months as an independent company.

"I'm a huge believer in constraints," Fake told me. "I really believe constraints breed creativity. If you have only a piece of string, a pile of sand, the phone number of a butcher in Aleppo, and thirty Argentinean dollars, can you get from Cambodia to Detroit? I'm sure it can be done."

Game Neverending was a tough sell; people weren't yet used to Web games or to nonlinear adventures. But the small Ludicorp team worked relentlessly, iteratively improving the product. They figured that if they added players incrementally, they would eventually accumulate enough customers to raise money, polish the game more, and turn profitable.

But venture capitalists were even more confused by Game Neverending than were consumers. Most games were sold on CDs or cartridges; Game Neverending was Web based. Most games involved straightforward missions and goals; Game Neverending was nonlinear and exploratory. Fund-raising was as grueling as it was fruitless.

"Now you throw a rock and hit a company building a social game, but this was not something venture capitalists understood at the time," Fake said. "Investors would ask, 'Can you buy the game at CompUSA? Can you play Solitaire on it?' Casual games were virtually unknown and understood as Tetris or Solitaire. . . . The entire time was frustrating. . . . No money was anywhere."

Game Neverending did have a following of hard-core devotees, but not enough to stave off financial reality. Ludicorp had nearly depleted its seed capital by December 2003. The game, still in beta, was nowhere near complete, much less profitable. The writing was on the wall.

But there was an idea floating around the office of how the company might be saved. It came from Ludicorp's front-end development team. In the rush to try to finish Game Neverending, their code, the part displayed in people's Web browsers, had zoomed well ahead of the game's back end, which lived on the company's servers. From their boredom, an idea emerged: Why not spin out the instant-messaging technology already baked into Game Neverending and do something novel with it? Instant-messaging programs were, at the time, all about text. There seemed to be a need for a program that transplanted Game Neverending's immersively graphical way of socializing into the real world. This idea, which ultimately evolved into Flickr, was the basis for Ludicorp's fateful referendum.

That Ludicorp's founders even considered putting the direction of their entire company to an *employee vote* spoke to their extreme faith in the creative instincts of their team. Providing creative freedom is a core tenet of the 20 Percent Doctrine, and Fake and Butterfield ran with the idea of creative freedom over and over again. When some of their engineers ended up with spare time on their hands, Ludicorp set them free to be, as Fake later put it, "restless hacker types," working in their spare time in true 20 percent fashion. While programming experimentally, they came up with the idea that would become Flickr, the one at the center of the company vote.

What Flickr was considering with its referendum was a "pivot"—a complete reorientation of a company around a new product or idea. The concept of the pivot has gained currency in Silicon Valley in recent years as tech advances continue to push down the cost of retooling. It's unlikely you'll be able to get your company to pivot, especially if (unlike Ludicorp) it's got more than a handful of employees. But the idea is still valuable. You should be willing to pivot your own side project when the conditions are right; if you're getting nowhere with your old idea and seem to have stumbled across one that's better. A side project pivot is especially well advised if you've attracted a significant number of team members and if they're enthusiastic about the change. As Fake and Butterfield showed, there are few better ways to get behind the creative freedom of your team than to put your future direction in their hands.

Pivots seem to go hand in hand with a common 20 percent problem: a sudden depletion of resources. In Ludicorp's case, the crunch was particularly dramatic.

"We didn't have enough money to finish the game," Fake told me. "Should we keep doing what we were doing, or should we try this photo chat idea? That was the vote." The photo pivot won 4–2 after a tense 3–3 tie, Fake explained.

"December 8, we started," she said.

The first iteration of Flickr, called FlickrLive, was written in an intense, eight-week coding sprint. It was beyond basic. More a lark than a product, according to Fake, it was basically an instant-messaging application that could push photo files to other people's computers, create groups of photo recipients, and form chat groups around the images. In other words, it was like every other IM program out there, but with the ability to send and receive pictures. Seventy-five percent of its code had been extracted from Game Neverending's IM system.

Just as Paul Buchheit had done with Gmail and AdSense, the Flickr team was adapting old work in a new and innovative way. This ethic of reuse is common among 20 percent–style projects. That's why the 20 Percent Doctrine says to build a prototype quickly ("worse is better") and to iterate new versions fast. Existing work contributes directly to the former by giving you a head start and to the latter because it's easier to work on and improve something you're already deeply familiar with. When you're launching a side project, always look for opportunities to reuse old work, as Flickr did.

The Flickr team definitely cared more about getting something out the door than advancing the state of the art.

"If you've released a product and you're not embarrassed by it, you've waited too long," Fake told me.

Midway through the development of FlickrLive came a stroke of luck that took some of the pressure off: a $150,000 interest-free federal loan. Ludicorp had been rejected once for the assistance. The founders sent the same application in for a subsequent aid round and, much to their surprise, were accepted. "On December 23, we got [the] letter from the Canadian government," Fake said. "Like Christmas. . . . Talk about a windfall." The money bought Ludicorp more time and allowed them to continue work on both FlickrLive and Game Neverending.

A rudimentary version of FlickrLive was previewed at tech publisher O'Reilly Media's Emerging Technology Conference in February 2004. It had been renamed simply "Flickr." The reception was warm; eWeek and the *Guardian* wrote about the prototype, with the latter saying that "Ludicorp's Flickr could become a hot site."

The first public beta of Flickr launched shortly thereafter. The team kept improving the service. The government loan bought only limited time for Flickr and its half dozen staff. Flickr needed to iterate as quickly as possible and hire as little as possible. This took a toll on everyone. Fake wrote on her personal blog that she worked fourteen to eighteen hours a day. "We didn't stop," Fake wrote. "We worked very hard."

The going felt especially rough early on, when Flickr couldn't seem to attract users, despite a steadily growing feature set.

"It had a critical mass problem," Fake told me. "It launched, dwindled, and nearly died."

"We got a thousand, maybe two thousand users from the Emerging Technology [Conference] launch, and were super happy about that. That was a creditable number! However sometime in March I remember becoming discouraged when our sign-ups dropped below ten people in one day. It was disheartening."

The feature that made Flickr really take off was the ability to upload a photo directly to a Web page, where it could immediately be viewed, rather than using special Flickr software to transmit the file to someone else's computer, where they had to open it manually.

Subsequent iterations let people add titles, descriptions, and comments to photos. Flickr's popularity was further bolstered when the site allowed people to "tag" photos with a list of keywords. Surfing tags became a popular way to find interesting pictures on Flickr. When the Australian embassy in Jakarta, Indonesia, was bombed in September 2004, early in Flickr's development, three different Flickr users uploaded pictures of the aftermath, all tagged "Jakarta." It was an impressive show of global connectedness for a site that, at the time, had just 60,000 users.

A dedication to fast iteration had helped Flickr cheat its near-death experience. Side project champions should take heart: No matter how moribund your product seems to have become, and no matter how apathetic your user base, every improvement you make brings fresh hope. Be a persistent, steady iterator, and you will be rewarded.

Flickr's tagging feature not only goosed user sign-ups, it also saved Ludicorp money. It proved such an effective system for categorizing photos that later, when Flickr was in better financial shape, it was able to turn away dozens of companies trying to sell it complex image-recognition software. The human-powered metadata from tagging proved to be more powerful than any software algorithm.

Simple, human-powered tagging gave Flickr a long-lasting edge over its rivals. Google has acquired at least three different image-matching and photo-facial-recognition software companies over the years to bolster its Picasa photo-sharing service. Even after all of that pricey tech, Picasa trails distantly behind Flickr and Facebook in total unique visitors, according to comScore and Quantcast. Like Flickr, Facebook uses a simple tag-based solution to categorizing photos. So let it be some consolation, as you struggle to build a successful side project with no budget and few staff, that your constraints may force you into simple, clever solutions that give you an enduring advantage over competitors.

Flickr's constraints also helped the company get in front of some helpful trends. Fake and her team didn't have the money to do market research, nor did they have some cushion of venture capital to allow time for advance planning. Instead, they listened attentively to their users, picked new features carefully, and rolled new versions of Flickr out as quickly as possible to get the feedback loop going again.

This approach helped Flickr benefit from the spread of camera phones and from the corresponding explosion in picture taking, which provided fodder for the site—people needed to put all those pictures *somewhere*. They were getting used to sharing personal information online as social networking and blogging became popular; sharing private moments on a public site like Flickr wasn't just for strange computer nerds anymore. Meanwhile, the spread of broadband ensured plenty of bandwidth for pictures, making it feasible to upload a whole photo album in just a few minutes.

These were trends that seemed to paralyze Flickr's more comfortable, better-funded competitors. Ofoto, Shutterfly, and Snapfish had deep pockets—each had announced funding rounds of tens of millions of dollars—but remained stubbornly focused on selling prints. They buried their customers' online pictures behind a log-in; friends had to make an account and remember their password just to see any shots. This fit the sites' old-fashioned business model. If people could see digital pictures too easily, sales of prints might decline.

The whole point of Flickr, in contrast, was to encourage people to share their photos as widely as possible. The company built a drag-and-drop photo uploading program you could install on your home computer. On the website, you could get comments under your pictures from your friends. You could submit your photos to be critiqued in special photo-sharing groups. There were groups devoted to black-and-white photos, nature photos, and particular cities. You could also set off on a photo scavenger hunt—there were quirky groups like "Squared Circle," in which people took pictures of circular things like plates, manhole covers, and buttons and cropped them into rectangular photos. None of these ideas took hold on the well-funded photo-printing sites.

Ludicorp's founders had few preconceptions about their business model. So when their steady stream of new features led to a user uploading frenzy, Fake and Butterfield recognized it for what it was: a revenue opportunity. Their users were telling them, in behavior and words, what they wanted: *more*—more space for photos and more bandwidth to transfer them. That would be Flickr's business: selling premium accounts to people who wanted to store additional photos above and beyond the site's quota. The premium memberships immediately made nearly enough to cover Flickr's expenses.

After years of fruitlessly begging venture capitalists for money, Ludicorp was suddenly in a position where it didn't need investors. Of course, that only made venture capitalists more interested: Unsolicited offers poured in, at one point reaching three or four per week.

Meanwhile, Game Neverending, still unloved by investors and without a critical mass of users, seemed like a waste of time. Already marginalized within the company, it was officially frozen in July 2004.

After taking some money from angel investors Esther Dyson and Joi Ito in September 2004, Flickr was sold to Yahoo in March 2005 for a price reported to be north of $30 million. In August 2011, the service added its six billionth photo.

Flickr isn't the only start-up to remake itself around a side project or to thrive on constraints. A podcasting start-up called Odeo had a similar—and similarly successful—journey. Unlike Flickr, Odeo wasn't poor; it was coasting comfortably on a $5 million venture capital hoard. But then an identity crisis hit. Odeo wasn't very good at what it was doing and didn't know where it wanted to go. So the company decided to impose some artificial constraints on its staff—to simulate a Flickr-like environment, if you will—and was rewarded with a side project called Twitter that became a runaway hit.

Odeo was, from its first day, lost. It had a vague charter to become a big player in podcasting, a technique for subscribing to radio shows on iPods and other portable music players. Part of Odeo's problem was that it was created by Evan Williams, who had made a small fortune selling Blogger.com to Google. Williams himself later admitted he had too much money for his own good when he started Odeo. "I screwed up several things," Williams wrote on his personal blog, "several of which I knew better than to do beforehand:

not focusing the product, building for other people, raising too much money too soon, etc."

Williams had more success with his impoverished prior start-up, Pyra, where he had built Blogger in his spare time. Pyra ditched its flagship project management software, which was supposed to be its bread and butter, in favor of Blogger, the first easy-to-use software for blogging. Then the dot-com bubble burst, and Williams lost his entire staff, along with his cofounder, Meg Hourihan. But he kept plugging away alone (and unpaid), improving Blogger and rolling out a premium version in a quixotic quest to save the company. After nearly two years of working on a shoestring budget, Williams finally struck gold and sold Blogger to Google in exchange for a tidy pile of pre-IPO stock, believed to have been worth millions.

Williams's near-death experience with Blogger was worse even than Flickr's near-death experience in early 2004, after the hype from its public launch wore off and before it had enough compelling features to attract even ten new users a day. But Williams survived with persistent and steady iteration, just as Flickr had and as Gmail had before that. The takeaway for a 20 percent founder is, once again, to stubbornly keep improving your project.

Williams decided to re-create some of Pyra's desperate energy at Odeo, hoping to unleash some left-field creativity and revitalize the start-up. Rekindling his Pyra-era obsession with side projects, Williams broke his employees into small groups and told each one to spend the day experimenting, even with ideas that had nothing to do with podcasting. His mandate took the idea of 20 percent time to a new level. Instead of merely permitting side projects, as Google did, Williams was *requiring* them. In another duplication of how he worked at Pyra, Williams also encouraged the teams to develop and prototype their ideas quickly in the days and weeks that followed.

Jack Dorsey, an Odeo engineer, came up with the idea for Twitter during Williams's mandatory brainstorming day. He described it to his teammates while sitting on a slide at a children's park, eating Mexican food: What if people could use their mobile phones to trade status messages with friends the way they did on Facebook?

Dorsey spent two weeks hacking out a prototype with Biz Stone, another Odeo employee and a friend of Williams's from the Blogger days. He was working quickly to deliver a minimal prototype just as Paul Buchheit had done, and just as Caterina Fake and her team had done. By March 2006, the system, then dubbed "twttr," was live as an internal tool. To provide compatibility with the maximum number of cell phones, twttr imposed a brutally Spartan limit of 140 characters on status messages—another example of a powerful constraint.

Early on, it became obvious that sharing intimate moments on Twitter would inspire both joy and annoyance in other users—sometimes simultaneously. One day, for example, Stone was sweating and grunting his way through a carpet removal project in his Berkeley cottage when a twttr message breezed into his phone from Williams: "Sipping Pinot Noir after a massage in Napa Valley."

Twitter was opened to the public in July 2006. Its name had been lengthened from "twttr" and it had added a way to update your status on the Web in addition to via text message.

But Jack Dorsey's core idea of trading very short status messages was still at the heart of the product. And Twitter, rather than podcasting, was soon to be Odeo's mission. It was the obvious way to go; Williams's experiment in forced 20 percent time had given a lethargic, meandering company focus and enthusiasm. In October, Williams bought out Odeo's outside investors for about $5 million and formally shifted his company's focus to Twitter.com.

In March, Twitter became the toast of the annual South by Southwest interactive conference in Austin, Texas, and tripled its traffic. Two years later, it had 105 million users, and is now somewhere north of 190 million users. Among the people who tweet are the president of the United States, Barack Obama; pop star Lady Gaga; and TV host Oprah Winfrey. Investors have showered Twitter with $1.1 billion and value the company at $8 billion. And it all happened because a company with millions of dollars from investors was willing to let go of that money, and the idea that had attracted it, for a hastily assembled side project.

If Flickr didn't convince you to be open to the idea of abandoning your long-cherished passion project and "pivoting" to a more compelling idea when one comes along, hopefully the Odeo-Twitter saga did. When he realized his podcasting project was foundering, Williams had the courage to throw the floor open to ideas from his teammates, bet everything on one of those ideas, and throw out the old project entirely. Anyone trying to make a side project into a phenomenon should be willing to be so brave when the right idea comes along.

3

The Rise of Hack Day

How Yahoo Popularized a Pressure-
Cooker Version of 20 Percent Time

In early 2005, a start-up called JotSpot found itself with a serious case of Google envy. The maker of corporate wiki software badly wanted to emulate 20 percent time—to empower employees to follow their passions, to make the workplace more intrinsically rewarding, and to figure out radical new ways of helping its customers. But JotSpot was just seven months old, small, and perpetually shorthanded. All its efforts fizzled. "In a start-up, it's very hard to introduce 20 percent time," former JotSpot VP and current Googler Kevin Norton told me. "You're always under the gun, and everybody's doing a little bit of everything, so 20 percent time ends up being 0 percent time, even with the best of intentions." JotSpot tried a bunch of different things; none of them worked. It seemed like every time the company allocated time for experimentation, something urgent would come up at the last minute.

JotSpot's Google envy persisted unabated until CEO Joe Kraus spotted an intriguing blog post out of Sydney, Australia. Like Kraus, Mike Cannon-Brookes ran a small software company, Atlassian. And like Kraus, he was fascinated by 20 percent time. "It's very intriguing," he wrote, but "letting your engineers run around wild one day a week is very scary indeed to any manager." So the Aussie entrepreneur came up with a compromise with his staff over lunch one day: His engineers could run wild *once* rather than one day per week, creating a prototype in eight hours and demonstrating it to the rest of the company. It would be a pressure-cooker version of 20 percent time. Referencing the concept of one-day delivery, Cannon-Brookes called his event "FedEx Day—a mini, experimental, heavily bastardized version of Google's 20 percent playtime." He was thrilled with the results, he said, which included a task list maker, a flowchart generator, and tools for updating and debugging Atlassian's software suite.

Kraus was sold, and less than two weeks after Cannon-Brookes's blog post, JotSpot staged its own version of the event, rechristened as a "hackathon." Not only did the hackathon result in features like real-time collaborative editing, drag-and-drop tables, and software triggers on JotSpot's wiki product, but morale shot up, too—the hackathon ended with air horns, cheering, and the enthused yelling of an engineer: "I just want to crawl into my hole [cubicle], grow a beard, and build shit!" Kraus immediately decided to make hackathons a routine part of life at JotSpot. "It's unbelievable what you can get done in a day with a focused, motivated, and creative team," he wrote later. "I honestly believe that *every* company could benefit from [hackathons]."

Soon, a great many companies *would* benefit from hack-athons. JotSpot's event hadn't just fired up one company; it had turned hack days from a one-off event in Sydney to a nascent corporate innovation. Enter Chad Dickerson, the laid-back, freedom-loving, rabble-rousing Yahoo programmer, a sort of cross between Bill Gates and cult movie character Jeff "The Dude" Lebowski, who turned a far-out experiment in unstructured programming into a global phenomenon. By following in the footsteps of Atlassian and JotSpot, by launching a long series of Yahoo! Hack Days, and by enlisting everyone from gossip bloggers to the rock star Beck to promote them, he turned hack days into a full-fledged juggernaut now embraced by Google, Facebook, Twitter, eBay, LinkedIn, and many other leading tech companies.

Hack days are like 20 percent time on crack. They are cheaper, higher-pressure venues for employees to work on their own ideas. They are also chattier affairs, in which participants are encouraged to show their ideas to one another, to managers and executives, and even to customers. For companies that also adopt more conventional 20 percent time policies, they are a gateway drug—an on-ramp where employees can prove their ideas with prototypes and get them promoted to full 20 percent projects.

For your own side project, hack days, as we'll see, provide a great environment for getting an initial design off the ground and for collecting feedback and inspiration. They give you a hard deadline and a shot of adrenaline when you need a burst of creativity. They can also help you get perspective and support from people outside your company. And Yahoo's Hack Day, along with many of the hacks it gave rise to, is a great example of the power of emotionally resonant products.

All those upsides help explain why, even more than 20 percent time, hack days are now everywhere. Here's how it happened.

Yahoo's inaugural Hack Day came seven months after JotSpot and Atlassian's. The company's first Open Hack Day—the Woodstock of hackathons, open to people who didn't work at Yahoo—happened nine months after that, kicking off a global phenomenon that has seen dozens and dozens of Yahoo! Hack Days staged across five continents. The story of Yahoo! Hack Day's leader Dickerson is one of cutting through and defying bureaucracy. The ways he short-circuited Yahoo's management structures and pushed the boundaries of acceptable corporate behavior stand as valuable lessons to any 20 percent organizer trying to make room for innovative passion projects. His attitude is a lesson, too, in and of itself. Time and time again, Dickerson pushed with an almost casual subtlety past people's expectations, making Hack Day ever more electrifying, more technically dazzling, more subversive, wilder, and more dangerous, even, than anyone anticipated. The low-key edginess he brought to the table—always deferential, always polite, but relentless and sometimes startling—were crucial to landing hack days the broader popularity that turned them from tech company exercise into a bona fide cultural force.

The original idea wasn't so grand. By 2005, Yahoo was in bad shape. Once the Internet's guiding star, the company had been eclipsed by Google, whose mammoth ad revenues were growing much more quickly than Yahoo's and whose technology had surpassed Yahoo's in such strategically crucial areas as search, e-mail, and contextual advertising. "Things were on a steady decline at that point," said Norton, who left Yahoo just as JotSpot was launching its inaugural hackathon.

A top Yahoo executive named Brad Horowitz, Dickerson's boss, thought he could help the company get its mojo back. He had a powerful ally in Jerry Yang, who was himself a certified hacker, having cofounded Yahoo when he was a Stanford graduate student in electrical engineering. Yang and cofounder David Filo built Yahoo with a collegiate atmosphere, caffeinated and collaborative, in which features were rapidly added to Yahoo's flagship directory service. The company was a hotbed of innovation. Then it grew, tremendously, and then the dot-com bubble burst, and then Yahoo was put under the control of Terry Semel, a Hollywood mogul direly lacking in technical chops. Horowitz wanted to recapture Yahoo's original, freewheeling spirit. His elite Technology Development Group, within Yahoo's search division, acquired Flickr, the photo-sharing site described in the previous chapter. Shortly thereafter, Yahoo bought Delicious, a site for sharing Web bookmarks. The two start-ups embraced the sort of agility Horowitz wanted to spread to the rest of the company.

The hackathon concept took to an extreme the sorts of constraints that made the small, cash-strapped Flickr team so successful. It also promised to advance Horowitz's goal of attracting outside developers to Yahoo's application programming interfaces, or APIs. After seeing it in action at Atlassian and JotSpot, Horowitz decided to bring the hackathon to Yahoo.

He was egged on by Dickerson. A veteran of the fast-paced news industry, Dickerson developed Web systems for CNN,

Salon.com, and InfoWorld, and believed deadlines catalyzed creativity. He also believed deeply in a "hacker ethic" emphasizing the passion and individual prerogatives of programmers and the cultural potential of coding.

"I was wondering, 'What happens when the guy who, like, works on, say, Yahoo! Messenger all day is given free rein to do, like, whatever?'" Dickerson said. "I've always found that good developers work on cool things when they're not given any constraints. . . . Literally every time, in many different contexts, that I've been in a situation where engineers were allowed to do whatever they wanted, they do amazing stuff."

As a "platform evangelist," Dickerson acted as a communications bridge between the internal engineers who built Yahoo's systems and the external programmers who built on top of these systems. So he knew Yahoo's engineers had great ideas buzzing around inside their heads; he'd thrown back beer with them, he'd chatted them up in the hallways of Yahoo's Sunnyvale campus, he was on their e-mail discussion lists. But their creative energy could never break through the company's labyrinthine org chart. Amid Google's gains and Yahoo's depressed stock price, Semel was on the way out; Yahoo would have three CEOs over eighteen months in the ensuing chaos. Yahoo's corporate strategy was in flux, to put it generously. The tumult wasn't something Dickerson could fix.

What Dickerson *could* do was show how much potential was bottled up inside Yahoo. He wanted people to uncork their ideas—to convert daydreams into demonstrations.

The idea of a hacking marathon had been jangling around in Dickerson's head ever since he'd heard of Atlassian's FedEx Day. He hoped a FedEx Day–style hackathon would give engineers a reprieve from red tape and encourage a new spirit of creativity and vitality. Dickerson loved the idea of delivering completed software applications overnight, of programmers working in frenzied teams, and of hackers showing off to one another their hacks—half-baked, sure, but ready to be polished and expanded if deemed worthy. The tight time frame forced people to stop imagining passion projects, to strip them down to their essence, and to rapidly make them real. And the presentations that followed, in which programmers demoed their hacks to one another, offered social support and validation even as they raised the motivating specter of embarrassment. The demos also gave managers a chance to review all the potential products rattling around in engineers' heads, gave engineers a chance to prove the potential of those ideas, and gave the best ideas the chance to become blueprints for Yahoo's future.

"We used to joke that the response of death from a product manager," Dickerson's Hack Day collaborator Jeremy Zawodny told me, "when you show them an idea, is that they would politely listen to you and say . . . 'That's on our road map.' It was a way for them to respond positively to you, but it means nothing. . . . Two years later you're wondering why the damned thing hasn't been shipped yet. Hack Day was a way to say, 'You know what? In twenty-four hours I can build it and show it to you, and I think it's ridiculous that you want to spend eighteen months trying to throw a product together.'"

Dickerson wanted to take the idea of a hackathon further than either Atlassian or JotSpot had. Yahoo's event would be longer, for one thing: twenty-four hours to Atlassian's eight hours and JotSpot's eleven hours. More crucially, Yahoo programmers would have total freedom in what they could work on. JotSpot's event required that the hacks be "valuable to the company," while Atlassian, which convened a collective brainstorming session ahead of FedEx Day, produced hacks that were entirely product oriented. Dickerson didn't want such a corporate feel. With more than a thousand engineers at Yahoo and just a handful of volunteer Hack Day managers, there had to be more freedom, practically speaking. But Dickerson also *wanted* to see off-the-wall, insanely quirky hacks. He wanted his programmers totally unbridled. "I really liked that it was essentially uncontrollable," he said. "Most businesses operate with some degree of structure every day of the year. So just, you know, relax for that one day and just be comfortable and, like, let it flow. Don't try to, if you're a product manager, look at it as a free day where you can get developers to do something on your project. It's all about shining the light on their creativity and letting them do what they want."

Dickerson was taking a core tenet of 20 percent time— that people are more innovative when allowed to follow their passions—and applying it to programming marathons.

Dickerson came up with a name to reflect the irreverent spirit of his event. Hack Day paid tribute to the hacker ethic articulated by tech author Steven Levy and open-source software proponent Eric Raymond. The hacker ethic is anti-authoritarian; the hacker ethic is about getting shit done; the hacker ethic is about working on things that matter to you personally; the hacker ethic is about improving the world. The hacker ethic is about as punk rock as programming gets. While Atlassian's FedEx Day and JotSpot's hackathon were like university cram sessions, Hack Day was more like an illicit all-night freestyle jam, with musicians riffing off and one-upping one another.

Teams would form ad hoc, well in advance of the event, without regard to Yahoo's official organizational structure. The only rules were to work fast and to work fresh—ideas from an engineer's existing to-do list were discouraged. Projects had to be finished within twenty-four hours. The idea was to do a burst of coding under a hard deadline. "It forces people to focus on just the most important things to get done what they want to get done," Zawodny said.

"You're setting some time and space to somehow be different, and that kind of frees up imagination," said thirteen-year Yahoo veteran Havi Hoffman, who helped organize subsequent Hack Days. "It's a little like institutionalizing 20 percent time. . . . By breaking routine you set up another dynamic."

Essentially, hack days remove some constraints while imposing new ones. Gone are corporate strictures impeding creativity. In their place is a kamikaze deadline. The creative freedom allows for the same sort of employee-driven passion projects we saw in chapter 1 under Google's 20 percent time. The deadline, meanwhile, acts as a forcing mechanism, stripping down and accelerating creative output just as it did at Flickr. You should consider using a hack day to develop the initial prototype for your 20 percent–style project, as well as to test new features. Even if your company does not offer internal hack days, the concept has spread widely, as we'll see, and there are now a plethora of hack days open to the public, offered by local hacker groups and at industry conferences. More broadly, consider some similar combination of creative freedom plus a tight deadline. See what you can create in a spare night, or weekend, or hour. There are all sorts of variations on hack day in the wild: some, like the three-day MashUp Camp, spread over a long weekend, and others that are more compressed. What all such events have in common is that they exploit the power of intense focus in a world that increasingly distracts us, and they leverage direct emotional pressure in a world that increasingly insulates us from our primordial survival instincts. Seek out anything that helps you replicate that focus and competitive urge.

Dickerson knew that marketing Hack Day within Yahoo was at least as important as the details of the event itself, and he made a concerted effort at internal recruiting. He started with an appeal to an internal e-mail list called "devel-random," a sort of virtual water cooler where thousands of company programmers exchanged frank chatter with one another. Dickerson announced his Hack Day plans to the list and invited people to join a new list he'd set up called "hack-discuss" for more planning and promotion. He later put up signs and even printed stickers that exhorted people to "follow Hack Day protocol."

"That was a fun way of saying, 'Don't bother the developers today,'" Dickerson said. "We really tried to make it seem special and subversive. . . . The language we used was different from the traditional 'bleeding purple' Yahoo corporate speak, and the branding on posters and such wasn't the traditional purple Yahoo stuff. In many cases, Yahoo wasn't mentioned at all. This wasn't about being unhappy with Yahoo—I thought things were awesome at the time—and more about making this event truly different: for hackers, by hackers, without the usual corporate sheen."

Not everyone at Yahoo welcomed the punk rock ethos

of Hack Day. Though the colleagues with whom Dickerson initially discussed the event were enthusiastic, some higher-ups wanted to focus it on company priorities rather than the free-for-all Dickerson envisioned. Dickerson saw this as a lethal threat to Hack Day. He pushed back. With backing from Horowitz, Dickerson successfully convinced the senior managers to back down from their proposed restrictions.

"I didn't want to poison the well with other people saying, 'This is what it should be about,'" Dickerson said. "In a company setting, the lack of structure is the whole point."

Zawodny felt the same way. "There were people that came up with things they thought were helpful suggestions to guide the hackers, but who totally missed the point of what the event was about," he said. "We did have to be strong about pushing back and saying, 'No, this works because there aren't many rules.'"

Hack Day began late in the afternoon on a Thursday in a central conference room kept well stocked with beer, soda, and pizza. Participants gathered again Friday morning for coffee, snacks, and last-minute questions. Hard-core participants had been working all night; most people went home Thursday night to get some rest. Then the teams went off—to desks, conference rooms, wherever they wanted—to hack out their code. They stopped late in the afternoon.

At the end of the day Friday, people demonstrated their hacks to everyone else. All the team presentations could easily drag on forever, so organizers took to cutting people off after two minutes with a special gong. The demo time limit would become part of the DNA of all future Hack Days, spreading well beyond Yahoo.

Dickerson hadn't known what to expect for the first Hack Day; he'd thrown himself into generating excitement for the event and worried no one would show. But Hack Day was a success; demos were met with exuberant applause and cheers, and then a series of giddy posts on the personal blogs of various Yahoo engineers, praising the outpouring of ideas, enthusiasm, and actual working code that came out of the event.

And far from being a snooze, the inaugural Hack Day actually proved *too* wild. Dickerson had to accept intervention from Yahoo executives over a hack called "Backyard War." It was sort of like the famous website "Hot or Not": Two employee pictures chosen at random from the Yahoo intranet, called "Backyard," popped up on your computer screen, and you were supposed to pick the "winner" of the "battle." No one had any idea how they were supposed to decide who "won," but everyone loved Backyard War, nonetheless. Well, almost everyone.

"The first Hack Day was a huge success, and the next day my phone rang and it was someone in HR at Yahoo," Dickerson said. "I thought they were calling me to congratulate me and the team on doing this great event. But they were calling me to say, 'You need to take Backyard War down. . . .' That was a little edgy in a corporate environment."

He complied, but Dickerson was over the moon about Backyard War. It helped make Hack Day fun, even a bit dangerous. It underlined that the event was about freedom—you were free enough to get yourself in trouble. "I think [it] kind of helped set the spirit of the event," Dickerson said. He saw to it that Backyard Wars' creator, Cal Henderson, took home an award for most unexpected hack.

Henderson, who had worked at Flickr before it was bought by Yahoo, was irrepressible. At the next Hack Day, he demoed "Who's the Boss?," which displayed pictures of two Yahoo employees, plucked again from the Backyard intranet, and made you guess which one was the boss of the other. You would then find out whether you were right, and which subordinates were most often mistaken for bosses and vice versa.

"I think HR may have called about that and shut it down," Dickerson said, "but at that point we were kind of like, 'Ha, ha! Which app's going to get shut down this time?'" Subversive projects became a constant part of Hack Day. Dickerson and the other organizers even came up with a special prize for them: "Most Likely to Be Shut Down by HR." Hack Day was as much about making your colleagues laugh as it was about impressing them. "The engineer/developer culture is actually very creative," entrepreneur and Yahoo! Hack Day winner Tarikh Korula said, "but creative in its own way. Not like fine art—closer to Monty Python."

Humor helped ease the pressure at Hack Day. Programmer Mo Kakwan, for example, found his Hack Day "delusions of grandeur" shattered when he fell asleep and was ditched by his teammates. The hack he threw together the next day was shoddy and haphazard. But it was also hilarious. Kakwan won over the Hack Day crowd with an off-kilter demo that retold his surreal late-night experience with his former teammates— their visions of making "the best hack ever," the rounds of high fives, and the moment when Kakwan blinked and "this blink ended being two hours long. I woke up at around six A.M., and my partner wasn't there, and neither was the other partner. I was freaking out a little. I didn't know what to do."

Kakwan then showed off the fruits of his labor, a system for creating a talking picture, in which you clicked anywhere on a photo to add moving "lips" and talked into a microphone, making the "lips" move in sync with your voice. For the coup de grâce, Kakwan used the system to carry on a conversation with a picture of Patrick Stewart, the *Star Trek* actor. "Hey, you're amazing—you should get the free TV!" Kakwan-as-Stewart said via the picture. "Thanks, Patrick Stewart! Make it so!" Kakwan-as-Kakwan replied. "It looks like magic but it's not," Kakwan told the crowd, tongue in cheek. "It's just Flash." The crowd roared, Kakwan took home the "Best Shtick" award, and a video of the demo subsequently racked up 61,000 views on YouTube.

As we've seen time and again, Hack Day had a way of connecting with people emotionally. Dickerson did everything he could to encourage this, from supporting subversive projects with the "Most Likely to Be Shut Down by HR" award to staging a rock concert (more on that later) to turning demos into boisterous moments of affirmation. We'll see later how emotional resonance was also employed by chef Thomas Keller to delight customers and by Huffington Post's Off the Bus to attract and retain volunteer writers. For now, you should think about how your own side project can appeal to your users' and prospective teammates' humanity, how it can hack people's feelings and create a special bond. As Hack Day showed, that can be as simple as allowing a little goofiness. It also means not being afraid to color outside the lines a little, to violate the letter of corporate policy in the spirit of getting people excited about their innate creativity. A little defiance helped Dickerson's Hack Days, just as it helped Paul

Buchheit's AdSense. It can be your ally, too, when it comes to making emotional connections.

The success of the first Hack Day opened doors within Yahoo. "I immediately had access to, like, every top executive," Dickerson said. He seized on his newfound power to expand Hack Day, turning it into a progressively larger event in the course of just a couple of years.

The first Hack Day, in December 2005, was followed by a second one the following March, this time with a more impressive array of company brass serving as judges, and another at Sunnyvale headquarters in June 2006. Then in September 2006, Hack Day really ballooned: Dickerson invited programmers from outside Yahoo to apply for one of five hundred slots to the first public Hack Day, where participants would be allowed to pitch tents in the grass around Yahoo's headquarters. The event was dubbed Open Hack Day.

Even as Yahoo network engineers raced to erect eighteen new wifi access points to handle the programmer influx, Dickerson fretted. What if no one showed up? The event was planned only three weeks in advance; Dickerson was desperate for some buzz. "I love spectacles and rock and roll," he said later. "We were sitting in a conference room at Yahoo, and there was a copy of *Wired* magazine on the table and Beck was on the cover. And I was like, 'You know what, we should totally blow this out. . . .' I thought Yahoo had the ability to do a really awesome event that would be more than a little mindblowing—Beck show! Camping on the lawn! Free beer all night!—and I thought that would be a good thing for the company's mojo."

Alt rocker Beck would be perfect for Open Hack Day. He

was a tech head, allowing people to create their own mixes of his songs on his website, releasing songs built from video game sounds, and conceiving a "visual version" of one album for distribution on YouTube. And he was slated to play the nearby Shoreline Amphitheatre in Mountain View the day after Hack Day. Horowitz saw the same *Wired* cover in an airport newsstand and resolved to get Beck involved. He quickly tapped the head of Yahoo! Music, former Beastie Boys digital guru Ian Rogers, to try to use his connections into the recording industry to land the booking.

While Yahoo higher-ups were negotiating with Beck's people, Dickerson and Horowitz made a risky and unauthorized ploy for attention: They leaked to *TechCrunch*, the widely read Silicon Valley blog, that a "special musical guest" would play on Hack Day. It was a career-endangering end run around Yahoo PR, but Dickerson and Horowitz were determined to broaden and diversify Hack Day, and to do that they needed publicity. "It was a concept at that point," Dickerson told me. "We announced 'special entertainment' without knowing that we would have it. . . . It could have just as easily been a lesser band, but we wanted to do something awesome, and announcing it in advance put pressure on us to deliver, which I liked.

"I think only Bradley and I knew about it at that point," Dickerson continued. "And I recall Bradley telling me to publish the [Hack Day] site. I think I was standing beside him when he leaked it, and the first call we got was from Yahoo PR. It's possible that we could have been fired, but I think we thought it was so cool that it would be silly for that to happen. . . . As we explained what we were doing, we got really strong support and everyone started to pitch in. I really don't think it would have gotten off the ground if we had gone through proper channels."

Applications spiked after *TechCrunch*'s post, and soared further when the site ran a leaked picture of an equipment crate on the Yahoo campus marked BECK.

Yahoo sealed its contract with Beck just six hours before the scheduled show time, with the roadies already setting up the stage (Yahoo originally just asked for a few acoustic numbers in the company cafeteria, but Beck wanted to set up his full stage show, and Yahoo was happy to oblige). The show was a hit, and Beck played well beyond his agreed minimum performance time, and even toured Open Hack Day, checking out what the teams were working on.

A heady energy infused Open Hack Day participants in the wake of Beck's performance. Dickerson had successfully fused rock-and-roll cool to the nerdy glory of a programming event.

"The phone booths in 'URLs,' the cafeteria that was the center of the action, reeked of pot smoke after that night," Dickerson said. "I recall a prominent Yahoo exec coming up to me that night and saying, 'Oh my God—people were hotboxing in the phone booths!' This was said with a certain amount of wonderment and glee."

In the hacking frenzy, some fourteen kegs of beer were consumed, along with four hundred pizzas. Fifty-four different hacks were demoed to a crowd of around four hundred; seventeen of them were honored with awards. Self-described "fashion nerd" Diana Eng and her team took the grand prize with a handbag that uploaded pictures to Flickr as you walked; the camera and pedometer were built in. Other winners included Road Trip Radio, an online map that gave you, along with driving directions, a list of NPR stations along your driving route and places where you should switch from one station to another; and Korula's Ybox, a small device that sent to any television a customized stream of Yahoo data, including weather forecasts, stock quotes, and Flickr slideshows.

The outpouring of good reviews—a flood of blog posts written by Yahoos, outside programmers, and technology journalists, including an exuberant report from *TechCrunch* publisher Mike Arrington—was like the buzz that greeted the first, internal Hack Day, multiplied by ten. Yahoo's first Open Hack Day was basically the Woodstock of hackathons. "Yahoo Hack Day was off the hook," one non-Yahoo participant wrote on his blog. "It pretty much set the bar for any future events like this." "Yahoo is punk rock," wrote another outsider blogger, noting that he had "never been that enamored of Yahoo" before. "It far surpassed anything I was expecting," blogged another.

Beyond the PR and morale benefits, opening Hack Day to outsiders helped Yahoo broaden its thinking about its own technology. "The internal Hack Days often had a smattering of hacks that would only make sense to folks who work inside Yahoo, like projects around internal tools, the company directory, etc.," Dickerson said. The Open Hack Day, in contrast, brought the worlds of fashion and music into the company.

Because they happen within the span of twenty-four hours rather than over weeks or months, hack days are especially well suited to bringing in outside observers, including company partners.

For its seventeenth FedEx Day recently, Atlassian brought in four customers from "a very large bank down the road," CEO and founder Cannon-Brookes told me, and let them watch the final hack demos and award a special "customer prize." They ended up picking a feature that had come in fourth out of six finalists among Atlassian's own judges, a modification to Atlassian's corporate software that let users delete from their screens input fields they never used. "Those four customers said, 'Look, all the other cool stuff like the videos and everything else was awesome, but at my job every day, I would like *that*," Cannon-Brookes told me. "They just had a ball, and they got to drink with the engineers and hang out. They got up and talked for five or ten minutes from a customer's perspective. What was interesting—and what was useful—was how the hundred and fifty engineers watching were thinking, 'Oh, okay, I wouldn't have thought of that.' "

Where hack days offer a 20 percent innovator the opportunity to get her ideas in front of her bosses quickly and cheaply, then, *open* hack days offer an even more rigorous sort of evaluation, a chance to show ideas to potential customers and to allow internal programmers to compare their work with hacks from outside programmers. Open hack days are really the ultimate sort of crucible for shaping, hardening, and proving the idea for a great 20 percent project. The opportunities they offer for outsider validation and customer service make them potentially easier sells to bosses who are otherwise resistant to the idea of 20 percent time or even to the idea of closed, internal hack days.

Open hack days also fit neatly with the 20 Percent Doctrine principle that you should embrace outsiders. You don't actually have to organize your own open hackathon to get that exposure to outside perspectives. Participating in someone else's hack day, like those staged by tech groups in San Francisco, Boston, and Brooklyn, and at conferences like TechCrunch Disrupt, is a great way to get side project feedback and inspiration from people outside your usual circle. The events can also be great for recruiting users and helpers.

In addition to Open Hack Day, Yahoo broadened the event further by taking it global. The international Hack Days, many of them open to non-Yahoos, proved to be some of the company's most popular and energetic events. Yahoo found that 20 percent principles could work across all kinds of cultures.

First came Bangalore, in April and July 2006, then London, and eventually São Paulo, Taipei, and other international Yahoo offices. Dickerson was nervous about whether the freewheeling spirit of Hack Day would translate to cultures outside the United States. What he found was that the hacker ethic was global. "I went to run the first [Yahoo] Hack Day in India, which was really eye-opening," Dickerson said, "because I realized that the only difference in the way the whole thing went was that there was different food. But [it had] the same structure, and the same way that people were passionate and excited and enjoyed this freedom from constraints and just delivered cool stuff." If anything, Hack Day was received even *more* enthusiastically; the Bangalore event was so popular, Hoffman said, that Yahoo had to turn people away. It was the same in London, where programmers at the June 2007 Hack Day kept working straight through an electric outage, caused when the retractable roof at Alexandra

Palace inadvertently opened up in the rain. A lightning strike had taken out the palace's fire-suppression system and the roof opened automatically as a precaution.

"People were like 'Oh God!'" Dickerson said. "And there were people finding tarps and throwing them over the expensive equipment. But within twenty, thirty minutes, we just got everyone together, into a dry area. We said, 'We're gonna get the power back on.' And people started using paper, just continuing hacking the only way they knew how."

Going global helped Hack Day pay off for Yahoo. The company continued to reap PR and marketing benefits, sure, but Hack Day also helped Yahoo find and screen companies to acquire. Yahoo first met the people behind the Indonesia-based social network Koprol at a Hack Day in Jakarta before later buying the company. Copout, a webmail system Yahoo bought for $20 million, was already in Yahoo's crosshairs for a deal but bolstered their chances when people from the company who came to Hack Day did "some really cool work and got some more visibility," Hoffman said.

Hack Day also produced tangible products for Yahoo, from mashups to new interfaces to advanced research, like a tool called Yahoo! Tech Buzz, which tried to predict the future using an electronic market where people placed bets on competing outcomes. Among the internal Yahoo innovations sparked by Hack Day was an advanced new method of searching Yahoo! Mail (dubbed "Hulka"); a new brand of local websites called "Our City" that mashed together photos, event information, locally relevant bookmarks, and loads of other data; a new authentication system (BBAuth) that Yahoo used to rope outside websites into its network; new export formats and developer interfaces (APIs) for Flickr and Yahoo! Photos; and new tools for the PHP (hypertext preprocessor) and .NET programming languages.

Atlassian found similar success; it now convenes FedEx Day quarterly and has gleaned a barrage of new features over the course of its nineteen Hack Days. JotSpot similarly reaped rewards from its hackathons before the company was acquired by Google in 2006.

Hack Days also provide intangible benefits to employees and companies. "Beyond the innovations that come from it," Cannon-Brookes said, "telling people to pause what they're doing, spend twenty-four hours exploring new things in a free environment, share and learn from everyone else's explorations, and then go back to your day job—I think the morale boost that comes from that is big. And when you go back to your day job, the way you *think* about the product and the customer and everything else changes."

Hack Days had a similar positive effect on morale at Yahoo. Zawodny told me it "was a timely reminder, every quarter, of all the creativity and capability we had within the company . . . especially when in the larger public sphere Yahoo was being beaten down in the press."

Hack Days did more than make employees *feel* good; they also helped them slice through layers of management. In the same way they short-circuit product development processes, Hack Days short-circuit the org chart. It's not just that participants can work on unapproved hacks; they also get to put their projects in front of company brass. That's the sort of exposure any 20 percent instigator should bodily ache for.

At Yahoo, cofounders Jerry Yang and David Filo were

involved as judges from the first Hack Days, and successive CEOs Terry Semel, Yang, and Carol Bartz participated as well, along with other senior executives like chief product officer Ash Patel and executive vice president Jeff Weiner.

"The idea that you're going to present to the entire company is important," said Flickr cofounder Caterina Fake, who ran Horowitz's Technology Development Group and helped run Hack Day after her company was acquired by Yahoo. "All the C-level execs participated, at least in a judging capacity. Some of them submitted hacks as well. It's important if a Hack Day is going to succeed that the big cheeses at the company participate, too."

Of course, it can be awkward when polished, extroverted executives collide with geeky programmers several rungs below them. Anyone using a Hack Day to try to sell a 20 percent project is well advised to rehearse their demo, or to ask the sales staff for presentation tips. Failing that, just keep trying—hack days are great for overcoming public speaking fears.

"I remember the first Hack Day," Dickerson told me, "there were some people whose hands were shaking, they could barely explain what they were doing because they had never spoken in front of 150 people in a room. And in an atmosphere that was like an NBA basketball game. It was unbelievable. People were like going, 'Yeah! That's awesome! Yeah!' It was a really energizing room.

"Someone's literally holding a clock and you've got two minutes to explain something you've been working on all day. You're kind of sleep deprived. They were really, really nervous. But what I noticed over time is that people started practicing the speaking part. And, you know, a year later, people were coming up, it's like, smooth. They became better presenters and better speakers."

At Atlassian, cutting through bureaucracy to upper managers starts at FedEx Day but can continue long after. The creators of some of the best FedEx Day projects are given "get out of work free days" by product managers who want to see them refine and then deploy their projects. "He may come from another team, [the manager] may not even control him," Cannon-Brookes said. "Stealing someone across the company creates a little friction sometimes." If there aren't any managers who want to give them free days, employees can take 20 percent time days to finish projects they are especially excited about.

Hack Days bust through conventional management hierarchies, but in their place they help build the sort of cross-pollinating, peer-to-peer communication flows that make Google such fertile ground for 20 percent projects, as discussed in chapter 1. At Yahoo, Hack Day project demos are now transmitted live to the entire company by a roving videographer and interviewer. Divisions have begun exposing more of their software functionality to the rest of the company via APIs, motivated by the desire to see their products incorporated into Hack Day hacks. "A business unit manager will be feeling down because, 'Gosh, I went to the last Hack Day and only saw two people build hacks with our stuff,'" Zawodny said. "And the engineers in the room would look at them and say, 'We need to build some APIs.' And they'd say, 'Really, that's all? Let's do it.'"

Atlassian has brown bag lunches a few weeks before each

of its FedEx Days, in which participants talk about what hacks they're thinking about working on and trade ideas with fellow programmers. A summary of the lunch gets circulated internally, another chance for pre-event collaboration. "It just sparks some early ideas and gets people thinking about it in advance," Cannon-Brookes said.

After Yahoo's Hack Days started generating publicity and online buzz, the company began to field questions from other companies. Sometimes other companies would contact Yahoo directly; in other cases, they would just vacuum up information about Hack Day from blog posts and press coverage and then launch copycat events. "When we started getting inquiries from people at companies all over the world," Zawodny said, "we said, 'Wow, we've tapped into something that goes well beyond Yahoo.'"

The march of companies following in Yahoo's footsteps and launching their own hack days has been impressively steady. Facebook, Microsoft, and Google now convene their own hack days, often referred to as "hackathons," and the microblogging service Twitter, which was born from a hack day convened by parent company Obvious Corp., stages hackathons for developers. Salesforce.com and eBay have also staged their own hack days.

"It's definitely an idea that works," *TechCrunch* founder Arrington told me. "We now do them at every [TechCrunch] Disrupt event. Total blast: The camaraderie. Competitive atmosphere but social. It's just very geeky and very fun."

Hackathons have also spread into the world of music and visual art. To take just a few examples: A Dallas musician began a monthly competition called the "Laptop

Deathmatch," in which participants have three minutes to generate a song using only a laptop and an external controller. A Boulder, Colorado, art gallery convened an "art battle" in which, every thirty minutes, a new word or phrase would be announced, and two painters would race to depict it. Chicago illustrator Ezra Claytan Daniels regularly convenes a "live art spectacle" called Comic Art Battle, in which teams of artists and writers compete in lightning comic-book-style illustration battles judged by audience applause.

"I do actually feel like it's one of Yahoo's most valuable and enduring contributions to Web culture," Havi Hoffman said.

For all its success as a cultural phenomenon, and despite sparking some interesting Yahoo products, Hack Day has not produced enough innovation to keep Yahoo ahead of the competition. In 2009, Yahoo signed a deal with Microsoft that ceded its search functionality to Microsoft's Bing. There has been a steady defection of tech talent from the company; all the major founders of Hack Day now work elsewhere: Dickerson is CEO at Etsy, Zawodny is CTO at Craigslist, and Horowitz launched and runs Google's social network Google Plus.

Which brings us to two healthy controversies about the hack day format that anyone interested in launching or participating in hack days should think about: whether Yahoo got the structure of the events right, and whether participants should be—or need to be—pulling all-nighters.

Hack Day "didn't necessarily solve the problem of launching cooler products faster," Dickerson said, "but I think what we proved is that innovation is not a bottom-up problem—sometimes you have everything you need to do really amazing stuff, it's just that process and top-down management needs to do its part."

Other Yahoo veterans agree that Yahoo has pioneered the Hack Day format while failing to make the most of it. The Hack Day's brightest days, in other words, are still ahead of it. It's an idea that has grown beyond Yahoo.

Daniel Raffel, a programmer and former senior product manager at Yahoo, has seen other companies do far more with the hack day format that Yahoo popularized. That's because, Raffel said, Yahoo! Hack Day tends to encourage "showboating" to fellow programmers rather than trying to create products the company could get behind. Part of the problem, he said, is that Yahoo's products are harder to use in hacks because the programming interfaces are chaotic— "abandoned, not worked on for very long"—in comparison to Facebook and Twitter's interfaces. "Yahoo wasn't an engineer culture," he said.

Raffel, who helps run music hack days and *TechCrunch*'s hackathons, thinks that if Yahoo had a stronger focus on engineers at the top of the company, as Google and Facebook did, its Hack Day participants would have created software that emphasized practical benefits over sizzle. At a recent Twitter hack day, for example, engineers improved the company's Mac software to download tweets much more quickly, using Twitter's newly standardized, publicly available streaming connection. "They eventually rolled it out in the Mac App Store as one of the most successful Mac apps to date," Raffel said. "That wasn't a project that was on their official road map . . . in a productive, healthy organization where you see hack days be successful, they turn into shipping code that other people get to use."

"Friendship Pages was a hack day project," he added, referencing a new Facebook feature that shows off all the public postings between two people and pictures of them together. "It's just a brilliant idea."

It's not just the culture of Hack Day that needs refinement; the mechanics could be tweaked as well. Douglas Crockford, an author of best-selling programming books and a Yahoo software architect, worries about the quality of the software that emerges from Yahoo! Hack Days.

"As a development methodology it's almost criminally awful," Crockford said. "The things that happen in Hack Day are not healthy at all. . . . You never do your best work when you're sleep deprived. . . . In addition to the sleep deprivation, there's the terrible food that you're eating and stuff. . . . In programming, so much happens in your head. The struggle over this twenty-four hours is to try to get it out from your fingers into a keyboard and into something that's going to execute and not fall over. That's a really hard thing to do.

"My biggest reservation about this is that software development for us is a marathon, not a sprint. We're trying to create the world's most popular website, and that's not something you can do in an evening; it's a much bigger thing. . . . Sometimes there is a lack of emphasis on long-term thinking: 'Let's just see what we can come up with in twenty-four hours and we'll go with that.' So it has encouraged the company to be—or allowed it to remain shortsighted in some of its activity."

Still, "while there are aspects that are not healthy, I think it is fun. So, if you could get a community that wants to play I think that's great. . . . As events I think they're a lot of fun, if you look at it as a sort of athletic event for programmers."

While Yahoo has continued to struggle with its overall strategy, there's no doubt its Hack Day has become a wildly popular model for fostering 20 percent–style projects, a model adopted by many of Silicon Valley's most innovative companies. As Dickerson once put it on his blog, "I've always been surprised at how intelligent people ascribe self-limiting qualities to organizations. . . . Large companies are 'slow.' Small companies are 'agile.' 'They' would never let us do this. What happens when you work in a large company and you are able to leverage the size of the organization to form a lean-and-mean ad hoc team with broad expertise (technical, management, legal, security, networking, etc.) on a moment's notice? Something pretty powerful—you turn the cynical 'they' who won't let you do anything into the unstoppable 'we' that won't take no for an answer. I learned that inspiration might be the world's only renewable energy source, and it scales like a motherfucker."

Dickerson's words are inspiring, but it's important to remember that "scalable" inspiration didn't erupt from Yahoo spontaneously; it had to be kindled through just the right social structure.

4

A Side Project School Rises in the Bronx

How Joan Sullivan Took 20 Percent Time to a High School and to a Higher Level

There wasn't much structure in Joan Sullivan's household. With ten children in her semirural New Jersey family, things could get chaotic. Joan's eccentric father actively encouraged this; the Jesuit priest turned Gestalt psychologist turned high-stakes poker player didn't believe in setting rules. There was no bedtime. He didn't believe in traditional schools, either, reasoning that they stifled creativity. He encouraged the kids to attend anarchic "free school" and romp around on the homestead farm the family tended near Princeton. "He was constantly trying to remove me from school," Sullivan told me. "He thought school would stifle my creativity so I had to argue with him on the merits of why I should probably go. . . . It was really the opposite of structure." This backfired: Sullivan not only stayed in traditional school, she resolved to become U.S. secretary of education.

Sullivan's father didn't succeed in making Joan allergic to schools, but he did give her a free spirit, a sharp mind, and an ability to meet intricate challenges in an anarchic environment. She would go on, starting at twenty-nine years of age, to create one of New York's most successful high schools right in America's poorest congressional district.

When New York released its first-ever set of public school "Progress Reports" in 2007, Sullivan's school, the Bronx Academy of Letters, ranked seventh out of four hundred New York public high schools, scoring a high "A" grade. Two years later, *U.S. News and World Report* recognized the school with a spot on its list of "Best High Schools." By 2009, Bronx Academy of Letters boasted graduation rate well above 90 percent, compared with the citywide rate of 52 percent. Even more extraordinary, the college acceptance rate was also above 90 percent. In its first two graduating classes, the school sent students to Columbia, Fordham, Sarah Lawrence, Wesleyan, Skidmore, Northeastern, and SUNY Binghamton. Its local success has been validated by upwards of $5 million in grants and unrestricted private donations to the school's endowment over six years, as well as additional money from progressive philanthropies like the Bill and Melinda Gates Foundation, which donated via the nonprofit New Visions for Public Schools.

"She really was a superb educator," former New York City schools chancellor Joel Klein told me. "She's been such a strong believer in high expectations. It really became the rallying cry for the school, in which they weren't going to allow the fact that they were serving challenging populations at Bronx Academy of Letters prevent them from getting consistently good results. . . . This is deep in her DNA."

As we'll see, Sullivan's high standards and uncommon confidence are not just important in inspiring schoolchildren and teachers. The high bar she set and the fearlessness with which she attacked her goals show how anyone should go about turning a small experiment into something bigger. There is a place for modest and tempered expectations. A 20 percent–style project is no such place.

Sullivan's school, the Bronx Academy of Letters, stands as an example of how a large organization can graduate beyond conventional 20 percent time, creating a pipeline that allows gifted employees to turn their experimental ideas into standalone organizations within the larger institution. The New York City school system looks very different from Google, but under reform-minded schools chancellor Klein it pursued a similar management philosophy. Klein facilitated the creation of many small schools with a diverse array of academic themes, and clustered these schools in the city's poorest neighborhoods—not unlike Google's multitude of small, fluid teams, its broad range of projects, 20 percent and otherwise.

Klein gave his small schools freedom to operate outside the tightly regimented rules that covered the city's older, larger schools. Much like 20 percent time projects at Google, they were driven by the visions of individuals; Klein gave principals like Sullivan wide latitude. They could hire and promote without as much regard for seniority. They could allocate their own budgets. And they could design their own curriculums. Like 20 percent project leaders at Google, his principals operated with minimal oversight. Klein held them accountable with school report cards, based on relative improvements (or lack thereof) in student test scores during the time they attended the school. "We transformed the principal from an agent of the bureaucracy to the CEO of his or her school," was how Klein put it in one interview.

Of course, the stakes were higher in the New York public schools than at Google. Children's futures were on the line. So New York took a more developed approach to hatching innovation. Klein's system was like 20 percent time in macro, just as Yahoo! Hack Day was 20 percent time in micro. Principals like Sullivan worked full-time, as did their teachers; for them the school was no 20 percent time project. But the staff enjoyed the same sort of devolved control that is the hallmark of 20 percent time, and as organizations the schools were effectively side projects within the New York school system. Among its most successful was the school started by Sullivan.

Sullivan came to the New York City school system with fervor for creative accomplishment that bordered on the religious. Sullivan always carried on her shoulders what she referred to as her parents' "big crazy dreams," their sense that the chaotic family they were building was "really important, as though everything was at stake." Her siblings had come from prior marriages before the parents merged the two families together, Brady Bunch–style. As her parents' only child together, the sole member of the family related by blood to everyone else in the house, Sullivan felt it was her duty to fulfill their hopes.

Her father worked as a writer and kept house, while her mother's photography and publishing business made her the breadwinner. *People* magazine profiled the brood in 1975 under the headline, "Feminist Pryde Brown Finds House-Husband Dan Sullivan a 'Wonderful Mother' of Ten." Much of the story was "fantasy," Sullivan said, but the ideal of changing the world stuck with her. "There's a whole story line [in *People*] about how this is a different era, there's a different role for women, a different role for men," she told me. "A different concept of family, a different concept of gender. I do think that I desired to be a part of something big like that, to make an important change."

As a child, Sullivan would try to "win" dinner conversations with her nine older siblings. Her competitive spirit served her well; she matriculated to Yale, earned All-American honors there as a lacrosse goalie, and, after graduating in 1995, went to work for New York's Civilian Complaint Review Board. In 2000, Sullivan signed on to Senator Bill Bradley's presidential campaign, an experience she reflected on in her well-received 2002 memoir, *An American Voter: My Love Affair with Presidential Politics*.

As she worked on the book, Sullivan began her career in education, teaching history at a public high school in the South Bronx. She was named a teacher of the year, a nice honor to put next to her favorable book reviews ("surprisingly suspenseful . . . and poignantly drawn," wrote *Publishers Weekly*). After two years working as a teacher, Sullivan began asking if she could do more good as a principal. "When I was working in schools, I felt like principals were a primary lever that was being underutilized," she told me. "Making sure we had effective principals leading our schools was critical to any reform work, so I became interested in that idea kind of unexpectedly. I didn't imagine myself necessarily making a career in the public schools. But the importance of the role . . . of principal became pretty important to me." Urban Assembly, the nonprofit that set up the high school where Sullivan taught, was going to create another school. Sullivan spoke with Urban Assembly's CEO to see if she could get involved. Sure, he said. But the proposal was due in two weeks.

Sullivan hesitated. She was young, inexperienced in education, and not even legal for the job of principal. It was audacious of her, with only two years as a teacher under her belt, to try to establish a brand-new academy. The idea of starting a school was, in her words, "crazy." "I didn't have my credential even to teach, . . . let alone to be a principal," she said. "I had a temporary teaching credential. I didn't have an administrative credential. . . . Richard Kahan, the head of the Urban Assembly, said, 'You know, sometimes the timing and the right life isn't perfect, but this is the unique opportunity . . . there is this incredibly important work to be done, seize the moment.' And so I did."

Sullivan agreed to write the proposal for Kahan. With Klein as chancellor, Sullivan saw a unique opportunity to create something truly innovative, unburdened by the usual red tape of the school system. Just as Chad Dickerson unleashed innovation at Yahoo by slashing through the company's bureaucracy via Hack Day, Sullivan hoped she could shatter expectations when freed from some of the rules governing most New York schools.

"In other circumstances, I might have gone into an existing school and tried to turn it around," Sullivan said. "But that's not the work that was going on in New York. . . . New

York was in the middle of a reform movement that basically said, 'We're going to take huge failing high schools and break them down into small ones.'"

Klein was appointed by Mayor Michael Bloomberg in 2002, the first chancellor installed under a new system in which the mayor named the chancellor directly and controlled the Board of Education. Klein and Bloomberg set about a sweeping and controversial effort to reform the city's schools, with a particular eye toward improving educational institutions in poorer neighborhoods. They imposed a system of tests and public letter grades to try to hold schools accountable for their performance, gave principals much more freedom to select teachers, and replaced many underperforming large schools with smaller ones. During Klein's eight-year tenure, he closed almost 100 schools and opened around 450 smaller ones like Sullivan's.

"We had three thousand kids, most of whom were performing poorly," Klein told me. "There was a lack of personal motivation—faculty would focus on the kids who had done well. The rest of the kids were kind of lost in space. And so there are a couple of things about small schools that really appealed to me, one of which was that they were created at a size that avoids the anomie at some of these big failing schools . . . [where] a kind of sense of failure had sort of imbued the place. Breaking that up created a personalization. . . . People know people in a class of one hundred and eight students or one hundred and ten students."

The cycle of closing and opening schools also allowed for an easier reshuffling of teachers, since principals could pick staffers fresh rather than go through the process of ejecting underperforming teachers at existing schools, which was much more difficult under the teachers union contract.

The school Sullivan applied to create was focused on reading and writing. She believed deeply that having the ability to communicate was a prerequisite to other academic accomplishments. And the literary theme fit well with Sullivan's background as a published author whose siblings include novelists Jenny and Martha McPhee. Sullivan was never completely sold on the idea of highly targeted education, yet Urban Assembly was looking to set up themed schools. Many of the city's other schools had narrowed the curriculum, discarding or reducing elements like, say, arts and athletics. Sullivan wanted to aim higher—to emphasize not just graduating students but graduating them into top colleges and exposing them to a broad curriculum. "A lot of kids are natural artists, or natural musicians, or natural athletes, so that's where they feel confident and validated," Sullivan said. A school of letters was just broad enough to accommodate these lofty goals while being sufficiently focused for the Urban Assembly.

Klein approved Sullivan and Urban Assembly's proposal in April 2003. Sullivan had just ten months to fund the new school, to hire the teachers, and to get certified to become principal—all while teaching elsewhere during the day and taking eight courses toward a master's degree at night. It was the sort of deadline pressure that would have been familiar to Caterina Fake at Flickr or to the participants in Dickerson's hackathons.

The school would go into the Mott Haven section of the South Bronx, in the poorest congressional district in America (excluding Puerto Rico), New York's 16th. Ninety percent of Bronx Academy of Letters students would come from families living below the poverty line. The school would operate inside a former middle school that had been closed for repeatedly failing to meet city and state accountability standards, and which was also notorious for a mini-riot in which the kids filled the stairwells with oil and the teachers locked themselves in their classrooms.

The academy had an open-admission policy, so it would not be cherry-picking its students. Some seventy-nine local children signed up to become ninth-graders. Many lived in foster homes or shelters, or were in the process of learning the English language. Some 60 percent were reading below their grade level.

Daunting as it was for a teacher with barely two years in the system to attempt to launch a new school, or for a well-connected Ivy Leaguer and member of a distinguished literary dynasty to try to do so in one of New York's roughest neighborhoods, Sullivan pressed forward. This took extraordinary boldness, a boldness that has become the hallmark of Sullivan's career and indeed her life. "I'm a person who has ample confidence typically," Sullivan deadpanned to me after I asked about her ambitious choices. The girl who defied her father's wishes to attend primary and secondary schools and then Yale became the woman establishing a school playing by its own, very different set of rules. For a twenty-nine-year-old, Sullivan had tremendously outsized ambitions.

This is the sort of confidence it takes to get noticed when you're working in the margins, when you're trying something different on a small scale—Sullivan started with just one grade—in an obscure corner of a larger institution. For people who believe in their idea enough to turn it into a passion project, Sullivan's confidence should be a template. What's the point of investing all your spare moments in something and then being meek about it? You need an obvious zeal for what you're doing and the ambition to seize big, daunting opportunities if you want to make your passion inspiring and contagious.

Sullivan found that getting official approval for her school was the easy part. Next came the challenge of finding good teachers to educate that school's initial class of seventy-nine ninth-graders. There would only be five teachers to start, but Sullivan knew that finding the *right* five teachers was crucial. To get into college, some students would need to improve their abilities by the equivalent of several grade levels in a single year, and Sullivan wanted teachers who could establish a rapport in order to get students not just participating but excited. It was a daunting recruiting challenge. But Sullivan was blessed with extraordinary flexibility in hiring and compensation. Most New York principals had to give preference to seniority in such decisions, even after Klein and Bloomberg successfully eliminated some seniority rights. But a section of the teacher contracts referred to as 18D/18G made an exception for new schools, which meant Sullivan had wide latitude to hire and promote based on her own criteria.

"People who are going to teach in the South Bronx or Watts are actually quite ambitious," Sullivan told me. "They want to take on the toughest challenges. But our teaching profession fails them because it has no ladder, it has nothing besides default tenure two or three years out."

Even when hundreds of résumés poured in, Sullivan was not confident she could get enough great teachers. Her initial five hires had a mixed track record. Some didn't work out and eventually left, but others would prove pivotal in the school's success, including Anna Hall, a former speechwriter who would rise quickly through the ranks.

The summer before classes were to start, the New York Department of Education allocated a relatively generous budget to the school. There was enough money to provide small classes, clean rooms, books, desks, and other things that are far from guaranteed in New York public schools these days, like staplers, lockers, and even a color-coded set of binders for every student. The allocation was, by the standards of the city, ample. Nevertheless, Sullivan began an intensive effort to raise private money for the school, money that would fund an endowment, capital projects, and operational spending on behalf of students, and that would eventually build a library, renovate an auditorium, fund up-to-date computers, good lab equipment, and uniforms. This was extraordinary even in New York, a city packed with well-to-do parents who take an active interest in public schools.

"My vision was, let's take the good practices that the charter schools and private schools are using and try to apply them to our school," Sullivan said. "A lot of the sort of entrepreneurial, private money that gets invested in education gets invested in charters. And there's a role for charters to play, but on a national level they're only serving two to three percent of our schools. . . . There is an enormous interest in public education. People want to engage; they believe in it even if they aren't sending their kids to public school."

Sullivan set up a board to raise money, stocking it with award-winning literary figures like novelist Michael Cunningham, biographer Robert Caro, and architecture critic Paul Goldberger. The school's fund-raising efforts met with rapid success, ramping to hundreds of thousands of dollars per year outside of grants like those from the Gates Foundation and any private money funneled through the city. "I hadn't heard of any other schools that did that, or had a board like ours, or that raised like us," Sullivan said.

The Bronx Academy of Letters opened in September 2003. The launch was not without its hiccups. On day one, dozens of the seventy-nine initial students showed up without the required uniform of blue polo shirts, black pants, and black shoes. It was an act of defiance; uniforms had been distributed to families well in advance. Students chose brands like Hilfiger and Nike over Sullivan's vision. For Sullivan, this was a defining moment. She was determined that the academy would not fold into business as usual. She did not give an inch. The principal sent every student not in uniform home to change. Those who came back again in street clothes were sent home again. It was a gamble: This was a group of students Sullivan wanted to excite and inspire, not alienate. But she also needed to show them that more was expected of them at her school. "It was kind of about challenging what came before," Sullivan later said of the incident, "and I think, for a [school] system, challenging a lot of failed promises."

Her high standards continued into the school year.

There were advanced placement classes. Inside the school, the theme of reading and writing was inescapable. There was a school newspaper and a literary magazine. There were weekly writing forums featuring professional authors. Keeping a journal was required even in math class; students had to explain in words their grasp of formulas and problems. Writers in residence rotated through the school, teaching intensive seminars. And bookshelves snaked through the hallways; students were encouraged to take books home.

But Sullivan didn't stop there. Her goal was to get her students into college, and this meant giving them experiences beyond the walls of Bronx Academy. Outside the school, students were sent to summer camps and to work on farms. Sullivan took her students to visit college campuses throughout the East Coast, and got them enrolled in precollege academic programs at universities like Princeton, Cornell, University of California at Berkeley, and Georgetown. She even sent them abroad; Sullivan later boasted that Bronx Academy of Letters students had visited dozens of countries on five different continents by year six of the program. "These are the things that open our students' eyes, light their fires, and ultimately change their lives," Toni Bernstein, president of the school advisory board, told me. The school hired two full-time staff to find external activities and programs for students to participate in.

"As a teacher," Sullivan told me, "I discovered that, with minor exceptions, none of the kids had been to any of the sort of rich array of cultural institutions or other spots in the city that were fodder for the imagination. I felt like we were saying, 'Okay, go to college, go to college,' and then ninety-five percent of our kids didn't know anybody who had been to college, and had never really been to a college campus other than walking by Hostos Community College, which looks a lot like their high school in the South Bronx. . . . I had

tons of kids in my class who lived in the Bronx their whole
life and had never seen the Statue of Liberty, who had never
gone to Coney Island and seen the ocean."

Broadening the students' horizons to new places and experiences was, Sullivan believed, crucial to their futures.

"What's motivational is understanding the sense of pos-
sibility that life holds," Sullivan said. "What's motivational is
connecting those possibilities to your own interests and tal-
ents. . . . The reason we study for the SATs is because we can
imagine going to college. The reason we worked hard in that
math class is because we have a sense of where we might be
able to apply that understanding in a career setting."

The way Sullivan started and ran Bronx Academy of Letters
should underline for anyone embarking on a 20 percent–style
project the importance of setting and enforcing high expectations. Time and time again, Sullivan refused to let preconceptions about herself, her school, or her students temper her
ambition. Despite receiving a generous budget allocation from
the city, Sullivan aggressively pursued private donations and,
beyond that, an endowment. When students showed up on
the first day of school out of uniform, Sullivan did not lower
her standards one bit. Nor did she see any reason why kids in a
poor neighborhood should be denied lessons from professional
authors, trips to foreign countries, or classes at Ivy League colleges. "I wanted to make sure they felt a sense of unlimited
possibilities," Sullivan told me. "The worst kind of discrimination we have seen in our school system is intentional and
unintentional low expectation . . . it's a really insidious kind
of discrimination. I've seen all colors, shapes, sizes, and ages of

people coming into schools and sort of saying, 'Okay, well, you can't do this.' "

I said earlier to be confident and ambitious about your side project. Setting high expectations, as Sullivan did, is a natural result of that sort of boldness. Officially backed projects can survive even when they are mediocre. A 20 percent project doesn't have that luxury. It needs to show excellence. When you're trying to get attention, you need eye-popping success. "You need to believe that's possible," Sullivan told me, "because people's intuition is strong, generally. . . . You change your team, and their sense that this is a credible belief."

With its accolades and well-stocked board, the Bronx Academy of Letters was able to go a long way toward meeting Sullivan's original fund-raising vision. In its first six years, the school raised $5 million in private funds and made news in the *New York Times* for being a key recipient of $29.2 million from the Bill and Melinda Gates Foundation that was awarded to various advanced New York public schools. SMALL BRONX HIGH SCHOOL NOW A MODEL FOR OTHERS was the headline. It used some of that money to expand, adding a middle school in 2007. It now has around five hundred students and close to eighty teachers and continues to rack up awards.

In late 2009, Sullivan accepted a job as deputy mayor of Los Angeles, with a focus on overhauling the city's schools. In a public farewell, Klein called the principal a "bold leader and forward thinker" who "served New York City and our students extremely well."

In her good-bye speech to the students at Bronx Academy of Letters, Sullivan was cheered enthusiastically by hundreds of her students. But she could not stop calling on the kids to do more, to do better.

"I have always received one criticism above all others, and that criticism has been the same, believe it or not, from the students as it has been from staff," Sullivan told the assembled academy. "And it has been, 'God, just take a second and give me some praise, just take a second to tell me all the great things that we've done. And I'm not going to do that right now. What I'm going to do is say for many years, I have walked through the halls and I know that you have cursed me both directly and under your breath. . . .

"And I'm not going to apologize for that to you, because I believe above all other things that the greatest gesture of respect that any school can give you as students is to hold you to the highest possible standard. This isn't just only for your benefit, this is for society's benefit.

"The future of this country and this economy and this democracy, the future of justice and equality and all the things that matter most depend on you, doing everything you can to make the success that you ought to of yourself. And on the same note, to teachers, they have always said, 'Wait a second, I have a ninety percent pass rate, can't you just stop and enjoy that?' My answer is, 'No, we can't.' We can't because this is urgent. And the thing that makes this work so exciting as teachers, and makes us want to stay in it, is that it's not done, it is not close to done. There is so much more for us to do to make this a society it should be."

5

The Huffington Post Brings
20 Percent to the Masses

Off the Bus Changed How We Elect
Our Leaders and Organize Ourselves

Until now, we've looked at employee side projects. In this chapter, we examine something different: a project that harnessed the spare time of people far beyond the host company, of thousands of volunteer contributors across the country. It was 20 percent time on a massive scale. Participants included students, teachers, actors, and computer technicians.

The project, Huffington Post's Off the Bus, was the first instance in which the idea of citizen journalism, in which amateurs report stories for free and bring the concerns of ordinary people into the news, was made to really *work*. By the end of the 2008 election, Off the Bus had changed media and politics forever.

"Before Off the Bus, no one believed that professional-amateur [journalism] hybrids could work," said Clay Shirky, the New York University lecturer and Internet culture expert. "Afterward, everyone did." As the *New York Times* wrote in the heat of the 2008 presidential campaign, "Off the Bus is now probably the biggest . . . of all the new political, non-candidate sites to spring up during the [race]."

Much of the credit goes to Amanda Michel, who commanded Off the Bus's daily operations. Her real-world experience organizing Internet volunteers for two presidential candidates helped her realize the vision of countless starry-eyed citizen journalism utopians who had come before. "Amanda's work on Off the Bus helped transform journalism in two big ways," said Shirky. "First, she showed that citizen journalism was not just possible but practical and, second, she showed that amateurs produce different kinds of value than the pros."

In chapter 4, we saw how Joan Sullivan's high standards created an academic oasis for children in the South Bronx. In this chapter, we'll see how Michel and her team convinced thousands of adults to voluntarily hew to standards no less ambitious in order to change how Americans follow politics. Twenty percent projects live and die on their ability to recruit people, and Off the Bus did that extraordinarily well. It also showcased how to work effectively with outside contributors.

Unlike HuffPo's many opinion bloggers, Off the Bus's 12,000 volunteer journalists were carefully groomed and organized into teams capable of highly coordinated journalism—real nose-to-the-grindstone reporting that produced major national news. Its "citizen journalists" broke the monster "Bittergate" story, in which Barack Obama said at a fund-raiser that "bitter" small-town residents "cling to guns or religion." Off the Bus obtained an incendiary quote from Bill Clinton calling a *Vanity Fair* writer a "sleazy . . . scumbag" for writing about his wife. It broke the news that Democratic voters had begun to care far more about health care and education than the Iraq war. It used an army of distributed citizen journalists to build comprehensive databases of donor influence, party policy evolution, campaign tactics, and campaign offices. It was first to report how Christian activists were paid to write op-eds in favor of Republican candidates; it unearthed a preelection anxiety pandemic among black women; and it exposed the sad state of John McCain's field operation, presaging his resounding defeat months in advance.

Michel's breakout success had a lot to do with the fact that she was a fish out of water at the Huffington Post, working in the cultural rift between journalism and politics. HuffPo's newsrooms in New York and Washington, D.C., operate in isolation from the publication's unpaid bloggers, creating stories through individual staff without coordination with outsiders. Off the Bus, in contrast, used a small handful of paid editors to orchestrate the efforts of thousands of amateur citizen journalists. Michel wanted to get as far away from the traditional newsroom model as possible. A long string of prior citizen journalism efforts had failed because they encouraged volunteers to become like unpaid full-timers, trying to turn them into what Michel dubbed the Ideal Citizen Journalist, who can work all day, interview like a pro, turn in crystal-clear copy before deadline, and do it all for free.

Michel thought it was smarter to adapt journalism to the lives of the volunteers than to ask the volunteers to remake their lives for journalism. That was how it worked in politics, where volunteer coordination was the norm rather than the exception. Michel's vision was to break down the production of news articles into distinct phases that could accept small contributions from an array of people. "You need to find a way to channel people's energy so they can actually produce something," Michel told me. "You don't have to be a writer or writing a full story." Not only would an adaptive approach accommodate people's preferences on writing versus reporting, but it also meshed better into their busy schedules.

When Michel arrived at the Huffington Post's New York editorial headquarters in summer 2007, the publication was in full start-up mode, growing fast and chaotically. "No one knew who I was," Michel told me. "They called down to the CFO, and I remember he had this look on his face like, 'No one told me you were going to need a fucking desk.'"

Michel had been hired by Off the Bus's publishers, HuffPo founder Arianna Huffington and Jay Rosen, an NYU journalism professor who had experimented for decades with ways to bring ordinary citizens into the news-gathering process. After sitting on a panel together at the Personal Democracy Forum conference, Rosen and Huffington resolved to build "the preeminent site of the 2008 election," as Rosen later recalled. Michel seemed like an ideal leader, having cut her teeth organizing young people online for Vermont politician Howard Dean during the 2004 presidential election. The technology platform she played a central role in building, Generation Dean, was instrumental in making Dean an early front-runner. She later worked for Democratic nominee John Kerry.

"Arianna had a conversation with Jay, and they made a very fast decision, luckily for us," Michel said. "They did something I think that very few publications would have done. But it happened so quickly that I think only a few people there knew the implications."

The idea behind Off the Bus was to reform how presidential elections were covered, focusing on the concerns of ordinary people. NYU would supply money. Huffington would supply readers and more money. And Rosen would supply his citizen journalism expertise, having built the citizen journalism experiment NewAssignment.net with Michel, with Internet entrepreneur Craig Newmark, and with the MacArthur Foundation. Rosen had also tried for years to sell newspapers on an early version of interactive content generation called "civic journalism."

"The *Los Angeles Times*, they have their political editor, they have correspondents, they have researchers," Rosen told me. "They have a team that's gonna cover the election. But *you* can't join that team, right? We can read what they do. But we have no participatory room. You could try to send them an e-mail. 'Hey, why don't you cover this?' But it's not designed for participation.

"That was the idea of Off the Bus: political coverage, by a team that anybody could join. And when we said 'anybody,' we meant 'anybody.' This is why Arianna's great. Because she doesn't care how closely this resembles traditional journalism."

The transformative spirit of the project was reflected in its odd title, Off the Bus. It was at once a nod to, and a rebuke of, the tight-knit culture of political journalists described in the book *The Boys on the Bus*, a behind-the-scenes look at pack journalism in the 1972 election. Unlike the boys on the bus, who rode around the country with campaign entourages, Off the Bus's correspondents would remain in their hometowns, where no carpetbagging political reporter could match their knowledge of local issues. "We wanted them to do what journalists weren't positioned to do, or were too lazy to do, or structurally couldn't do, to take advantage of opportunities not afforded to journalists," Michel said.

This emphasis on fresh voices made recruiting Off the Bus's most crucial activity. The project started with a big advantage: the Huffington Post itself. By soliciting volunteers on the HuffPo front page and through the site's e-mail newsletters, Rosen and Huffington bestowed upon Michel a massive initial pool of recriuts. "Immediately—literally immediately—we had a thousand people," Rosen told me.

A big pool of leads is no guarantee of success. Off the Bus wouldn't have been possible if Michel and her team hadn't created an amazing experience for their contributors. A pivotal lesson of Off the Bus is that a 20 percent project rises and falls on how well it provides such an experience.

Asking people to help with an experiment, whatever it might be, is really a request to participate in a journey. In politics, this request is known as The Ask, and Michel was a master of it, of getting people to say yes, and of getting the most out of them when they did so.

Michel had learned in politics never to take a volunteer for granted. "Campaigns are constantly trying to motivate and inspire people," she told me. "People have to understand that they are connected to a larger cause. . . . You're often asking people to do things that are not as much fun." It was the same at Off the Bus.

Michel's luring of a typical volunteer started with a solicitation, which might run on the Huffington Post or go out over e-mail. The format was always the same. "Our plugs . . . followed the equation that I learned on the Dean and Kerry campaigns," Michel told me. "It's very straightforward: The first paragraph is what we're trying to do. The next thing you do is give a link to sign up. Our next two or three paragraphs answered people's secondary questions: what might prevent them from doing it, how much time they'll need, why you need their help, why someone else couldn't do it, how this will make a difference. Offer the sign-up link again at the end. I learned and worshipped this formula.

"We gave people a sense of belonging but also a purpose. I think it was really important for them but it was really helpful for us. . . . Because sometimes you come up with something and it's like doing your first draft. You're writing [The Ask], and you're like, 'No, this is really not worth people's time. This doesn't really answer a unique enough question.'"

Sometimes Michel and her team approached people individually, recruiting especially active commenters on political blogs like *Daily Kos*, individual writers like *Blue Hampshire* blogger Mike Caulfield, or even newspaper writers like Linda Hansen, who penned op-eds for a small South Carolina paper. Michel found other contributors because Huffington Post editors regularly forwarded her calls from stray readers, knowing she was eager to talk to outsiders. Sometimes recruiting is as simple as answering the telephone. In an age of e-mail, Twitter, and information overload, it's an increasingly rare practice.

Michel's second step, once she had a lead, was wooing.

She would personally call each of her future contributors to answer any questions they had about Off the Bus, to determine what sort of work they preferred to do, and to gauge their willingness to invest time.

Next, Michel sought to close the deal. She made every effort to assign fresh recruits to "fun" first assignments. Such an assignment might be a speech by a hot candidate, or an exclusive fund-raiser. Some volunteers relished the chance to write opinion pieces, which Michel called Off the Bus's "gateway drug." Michel devised the "fun first assignment" policy during Off the Bus's debut reporting effort, Eyes on the Money, in July 2007, when she dispatched researchers to pore over campaign finance reports from the leading presidential candidates, looking for interesting activity. She hoped to leapfrog the mainstream media using Off the Bus's army of volunteers; the task of examining hundreds of pages of financial data, all available from a federal website, was one well suited to a large number of people with just a bit of time to offer. But the mostly liberal volunteers wasted time bickering over who got to cover the Obama and Clinton expenditures.

"No one wanted to be on team Ron Paul," Michel told me. "They would say, 'I'm not going to do this unless I can get switched to Obama.' It was one of the great ironies about Off the Bus: People were initially very concerned that we would pound the GOP in part because we were affiliated with the [left-leaning] Huffington Post. What happened is most of the big stories we broke were about the left because that's where people gravitated. They tended to be left and therefore they scrutinized their own."

Eyes on the Money was an exception. Participants

discovered that Republican Mitt Romney's campaign had an unusually high number of paid staff in proportion to its budget; it turned out that the Mormon candidate's campaign was paying Christian activists and other social conservatives to be "get out the vote consultants," an arrangement similar to "walking-around money" political machines used to hand out. An Off the Bus volunteer wrote about the payments with help from former *Washington Post* reporter Thomas Edsall, touching off a controversy that was covered in other news outlets. ARMY OF AVERAGE JOES CULLS THROUGH CANDIDATES' FILES, BIOS was the headline in the *Christian Science Monitor*.

Michel found that people who had a happy first experience, whatever it was, were more likely to stay on at Off the Bus to do the less glamorous work. In other words, earning seniority meant earning the right to do chores, not to shunt them off on others. "Joe Trippi would always tell us," Michel said, recalling her time working for Dean, "campaigns aren't just about what people do, they're about what they experience. You need to think about that a lot and how to create shared experience."

After successfully providing the volunteer with a fun first experience, Michel's next step was to find the person regular work that fit with his or her interests and skills. Then Michel would rope the hard core of her volunteers in further, enlisting them in elite Off the Bus teams like the Special Ops Squad.

Michel hoped the Special Ops Squad's name, inspired by Michel's Green Beret dad, would gin up a sense of camaraderie. Some contributors were so proud to be chosen that they added SPECIAL OPS to their e-mail signatures.

Special Ops set about creating profiles of each campaign's field office, complete with pictures, press contacts, and volunteer head counts. These profiles were kept regularly updated with fresh data. "It was, in my opinion, a perfect citizen journalism project," Off the Bus page editor John Tomasic told me. "It was a really specific task. And it was something no newspaper really could do, because we had people in every neighborhood around the country, practically: two thousand contributors going out to their local McCain or Obama headquarters.

"And the photos, these digital photos we got back, they told the story. This is like in June or July 2008 [four months before Obama defeated McCain]. The McCain headquarters: one gray-haired old lady, a phone that didn't work, and, like, a GONE FISHIN' sign. And then we had these Obama headquarters that were just booming with young people with cell phones and everything. And we knew, like . . . he's gonna win! The ground game is not even close. From the visual evidence. The reporters didn't have to do anything. They didn't have to depend on any, you know, reporterly skills. Get the evidence. They just told us this national story that was great."

Dan Treul, a Michigan college journalist recruited by Michel after she saw his political campaign coverage on PBS Online, was named to a different elite group, the National Correspondents, and worked on several other distributed reporting projects. "We interviewed hundreds of pastors around the country and visited the churches and surveyed their opinions going to the primaries," he said. The pastors "were much more diverse in opinion than what was really being portrayed in the national media."

Michel's recruiting process is an excellent blueprint for seducing people to help on a 20 percent–style project. In abstract terms, Michel did a handful of simple but highly effective things to draw people in to Off the Bus:

- **Cast a wide net.** Michel didn't limit herself to people with experience in journalism or politics. Everyone who read the Huffington Post was a potential recruit. Often, Michel's e-mails asked only for "political junkies" or people "adventurous, curious, and passionate."

- **Ask specifically.** Michel never beat around the bush, even when soliciting help from an audience of thousands. She communicated exactly why she needed volunteer help, for example: "Over the next two weeks the [Obama] campaign will be holding hundreds of small gatherings where the public is invited to help shape the nominee's platform." And she communicated exactly what volunteers would need to do, like so: "Would you watch McCain's speech in a public place—bar, library, college dorm, McCain Watch Party—and report on the crowd's reaction?"

- **Show them a good time.** Michel tried to ensure all volunteers had a fun first experience, even if that meant depriving experienced volunteers of plum assignments. This was in part a gesture of respect, a way of clearly showing a stranger his or her time was appreciated.

- **Get close.** Even with thousands of volunteers, Michel found ways to talk to people individually on the phone. Partly, this was to get a deeper feel for how they could best fit in at Off the Bus, and in part it was to provide a human voice behind the largely computerized project, and in part to help Michel craft tasks to her volunteers' capabilities.

- **Corral the elite.** Typically, the reward for being a great volunteer is that you're given more work to do. That's not always encouraging. But Michel put a positive spin on asking people for additional help when she created teams with elite status, like Special Ops and the National Correspondents initiative. Extra work is more appealing when wrapped in extra cachet.

Michel's recruiting skills transferred well from politics to Off the Bus. But after two months, she said, "it quickly became apparent that we really needed to have someone who could make some of those harder editorial calls, to think a lot more about our editorial objectives and editorial standards." Michel, Huffington, and Rosen brought in University of Southern California professor, seasoned journalist and longtime *Nation* magazine writer Marc Cooper as editorial director, based out of Los Angeles, where Huffington herself lived. Cooper would act as Off the Bus's journalistic leader and conscience. He was an eager recruit. "There was such a lack of urgency to these [*Nation*] folks," Cooper told me. "This was an exciting election and I wanted to report it in an exciting way."

Cooper was quickly integrated into the Off the Bus recruiting process. After Michel found people, pitched them, and signed them up, Cooper would talk to them about their writing to get a sense of how they might help with stories. He also began to recruit seasoned journalists as contributors.

Shortly after Cooper joined, around the same time as Eyes on the Money, he and Michel launched coverage of the critical Iowa presidential caucuses. Off the Bus deployed a large team of volunteer reporters to Iowa to offer comprehensive coverage. "We mobilized the biggest reporting team in the country," Cooper told me. "We had an organized crew of twenty or more people, and we coordinated it weeks in advance."

Roping people into Off the Bus with The Ask and fun first assignments and all that was one thing. Keeping them around was something else. The elite Special Ops and National Correspondents helped. But another key to Off the Bus's success was its ongoing contact with volunteers once they were writing and/or reporting for the site. Michel and Cooper convened weekly conference calls in which they answered questions and praised stories that had been well reported or had generated a lot of traffic. Writers would talk about how their stories came together. Michel and Cooper also sent out weekly e-mails about Off the Bus's progress, summarizing key stories, outlining coming projects, and listing who had been assigned to what.

Purely as a way of doling out work, the e-mails and calls had a mixed track record, Michel says. Sometimes people would go off and do assignments that had never been spelled out in the e-mails, or they would ignore key points discussed in the calls. But the communication was essential for morale. It reminded people they were part of something bigger than themselves. And it helped volunteers model behavior for one another. Michel had learned during the Kerry campaign that volunteers were much more likely to submit opinion pieces to their local newspapers when they read a firsthand account from someone else who had published one, as opposed to when they just read guidelines and a contrived sample editorial. "I appreciated the effort they took to really work with a core group of writers that would serve them throughout the election," Treul told me.

Without the momentum from its routines, Michel says, Off the Bus might have ended up like the U.K. *Guardian*'s distributed effort to sift through parliamentary expenses. The newspaper succeeded at first, recruiting thousands of online volunteers who reviewed more than 200,000 pages of documents, unearthing such unexplained reimbursements as $1,500 for food, a $330 pen, and $5,600 the prime minister possibly spent on a big-screen television. But then the *Guardian* was deserted by most of its contributors as the scandal subsided in the press; a year later, it was still seeking volunteers to examine another 200,000 pages of remaining expense documents.

As the campaign season advanced, Michel, Cooper, and Rosen took stock. Their ambitious citizen journalism project was clearly on the right track. But Off the Bus's leaders worried they were squandering the thousands of potential volunteers in their database. Many of those people, even the ones who had spoken directly to Michel and Cooper, were still dormant. How could Off the Bus make more use of these wallflowers? The answer, it turned out, was to make less use of them.

Just as Off the Bus cultivated hard-core members with elite teams, it also crafted projects that lowered the bar for involvement. After Iowa and the Eyes on the Money project, Michel and Cooper looked for projects that would be even easier for citizen journalists to become involved in.

One was called "Eyes and Ears." The idea was that contributors would file fifty-to-one-hundred-word personal stories about the election that resembled the New Yorker's Talk of the Town pieces. Maybe by opening Off the Bus to more topics, Michel and Cooper could get more volunteers to participate. It worked: In poured a flood of stories. Contributors sent vignettes from fund-raisers, accounts of rallies, and other scenes from the campaign trail.

One Eyes and Ears scoop revealed how the Obama campaign was, in a break with campaign tradition, raising money by selling basic pro-Obama merchandise like lawn signs and bumper stickers at a significant markup. That story emerged because lots of campaigners were writing into Eyes and Ears with bitter posts about how their Obama lawn signs had been stolen, and Michel was eventually able to deduce that they were so upset because they had been *paying* for the signs.

Another big Eyes and Ears story came later in the election. A University of Virginia assistant professor uncovered an anxiety pandemic among pro-Obama African American women after her doctor doubled her own dose of blood pressure medication and told her he had done the same for other black female Obama supporters. It was one of the Huffington Post's most popular stories.

Another Off the Bus feature designed to be easy on contributors was Road Kill, which aggregated bits of amusing news from the campaign trail. Off the Bus volunteers would submit short, column-style items into a wiki, and the best items would be woven into a column. Road Kill typically focused on fun pieces of minutiae: blog posts from Mitt Romney's family members, odd moments during press conferences, bloopers from the campaign trail, that kind of thing.

Perhaps the most successful example of Off the Bus lowering the bar was its Grassroots Correspondents initiative, which asked campaign workers to simply write about their behind-the-scenes efforts. More on that later.

One conclusion that can be drawn from Off the Bus's effort to lower the bar is that it pays to break 20 percent–style projects down into small, contributor-friendly chunks, and that chances are the ideal-size chunk is smaller than you think. Michel launched Off the Bus determined to atomize news gathering, and yet it took her months to realize that she needed to make workloads as small as they were within Eyes and Ears, Road Kill, and the Grassroots Correspondents.

Off the Bus thrived by lowering the time commitment required of its volunteers. But there was a much more surprising recruiting lesson in Off the Bus: You attract and retain people by giving them work that's challenging rather than easy, and by badgering rather than being low maintenance.

For all its efforts to accommodate volunteers, Off the Bus was suffused with high standards. When Off the Bus contributors messed up, Michel let them know. If someone failed to file their weekly campaign journal as promised, or did not turn in some campaign fund-raising research they had promised, Michel would call or e-mail to make sure they knew they had let her down. She'd emphasize that the person had committed to do the work and that she'd now have to find someone else to complete the task.

"We were a little nervous that that would backfire," Michel said. "But what we found in our volunteers is that that actually made it real. They were like, 'Oh, the fact that they could reject my content, then it actually had more meaning when I was published.'"

Michel knew from her experience with political campaigns that elevated standards were especially important for volunteers as opposed to staff. Without paychecks, the volunteers needed reinforcement that what they were doing was actually "real." Michel had been influenced in this regard by Kerry campaign manager Joe Trippi, who always insisted his people make their numbers, whether for fund-raising, volunteer recruitment, event size, or voter registration. "They knew which writers they could count on," one Off the Bus contributor, Dawn Teo, told me. And "they made sure that as their writers continued to write, that they were building credibility within the team. . . . I thought that was very important, because if you don't do that, then you're really just blogging."

Off the Bus's accountability went both ways, with management regularly admitting its own failures. When mountains of volunteer research on a particular project failed to produce any stories, Michel and Cooper worried the setback would prove discouraging. But going into painful detail about it, in a group conference call, had the opposite effect. Cooper explained to his team that professional journalists regularly invested time reporting stories that didn't pan out, which made the volunteers feel like real reporters.

Michel and Cooper also communicated high standards in more subtle ways. The original Off the Bus logo depicted a crappy, run-down old bus; Cooper campaigned hard to get it changed to something that looked more attractive. Michel thought Cooper was squandering his energy, but when the new logo rolled out, complete with a shiny modern vehicle, the volunteers couldn't stop talking about how happy the change had made them.

Off the Bus's high standards for its volunteers traced back to the high standards Huffington and Rosen had set at the project's conception—to make Off the Bus the most important citizen journalism operation of the 2008 election. "It was a very aggressive approach from the get-go," Michel told me.

The lofty expectations sharpened Michel and Cooper's competitive streaks. They wanted Off the Bus stories to land every single day on the Huffington Post's front page, a fiercely contested spot, and to get featured constantly in other HuffPo sections. Michel, based in the New York HuffPo newsroom, spent time every morning pitching other editors, placing Off the Bus stories in sections like Politics, Entertainment, Living, and Green. "It was a lot of persistence and it was a lot of sort of relentlessness," then-CEO Betsy Morgan said of Michel's lobbying on behalf of Off the Bus stories. "She was a good story picker. . . . She was well wired into what stories Huffington Post was interested in, what stories we were covering. . . . If [Michel] was feeding Arianna and feeding the editorial team—Katherine Zaleski, the front-page editor—stuff that was mediocre, then it would just become annoying.

But she wasn't. She was feeding really interesting nuggets, stuff that was resonating with overall coverage."

Michel's newsroom networking paid off; Teo told me proudly that she accumulated over one hundred front-page stories. Off the Bus ended as the third most heavily trafficked Huffington Post section, with 5.4 million monthly unique visitors, behind Politics and Entertainment.

The success of Off the Bus's high expectations illustrates a paradox 20 percent project leaders need to wrap their heads around: Recruiting is a seduction that, at its best, involves making a fun experience for participants, yet extracting top performance from your recruits involves being aggressively demanding and being ruthless in evaluating results. Michel's approach boiled down to being accommodating when figuring out how volunteers could help but, once their roles were set and boundaries established, expecting as much as she would from a paid staffer.

Although it held itself to high standards, Off the Bus went out of its way to feel more casual, more chaotic, less uniform, and thus more authentic than the mainstream media it was trying to disrupt. It worked. By being conspicuously different, Off the Bus commanded as much attention for its election coverage as the rest of the Huffington Post, at a fraction of the cost.

Off the Bus was eager to be different from the start. Early on, many volunteers submitted articles that read like traditional news coverage. Arianna Huffington stepped in to signal that this was unacceptable; she singled out for criticism a story about the Iowa caucuses by Beverly Davis, a seasoned journalist who had covered two presidential elections and filed regularly for the Austrian newsweekly *profil* and other European publications.

"Arianna was not happy with it because it was just too mainstream," Cooper told me. "The implication was that a citizen journalism project had to give you some perspective that wasn't otherwise available. And I think that's a reasonable conclusion."

Michel told her volunteers, repeatedly, that she didn't want them to imitate the mainstream media. Where old-school political reporters were trained to maintain a cold, objective voice and to hold the campaign at arm's length, Off the Bus contributors were instructed to be subjective, open about their feelings, and even, in the case of the Grassroots Correspondents, to get directly involved in electioneering. "We were always trying to break form," Michel told me. And she showed her volunteers how to do that, highlighting and promoting articles that embodied the fresh approach she was interested in.

Michel had been installed to run Off the Bus precisely because she did not turn instinctively to the routines of traditional journalism. This was why Cooper reported to Michel rather than the other way around. "I had tried paying some people with traditional journalism backgrounds to work on NewAssignment.net," Rosen told me, "and it just didn't work. It was much easier to take somebody who had an Internet background and teach them editorial than it was to take an editorial person and teach them open-source. . . . Professional journalism was never optimized for participation. It was optimized to keep people out. . . . It saw participation as the equivalent of interference."

There's a lesson for other 20 percent projects in the fact

that it took a political organizer to change journalism: Sometimes experience can be a weakness, especially if it binds you to old ways of thinking. Breaking the mold by putting Michel in charge led to all the other instances of Off the Bus breaking form: the personal voice, the partisan reporters (more on that later), the stories from behind closed doors, the stories reported by an army rather than an individual. Being different also lent Off the Bus invaluable buzz. The project maintained a high profile in the media, with a series devoted to it in the *New York Times* and partnerships with Talking Points Memo and Politico.

Off the Bus didn't just break the mold, it *looked* like it was breaking the mold as it did so. That's a great technique for any disruptive project. The self-fulfilling psychology of appearing different is why Joan Sullivan stubbornly insisted her students wear uniforms. It's why the skunkworks team that created the original Macintosh computer flew a pirate flag over their offices to set themselves apart from the rest of Apple Computer.

Off the Bus's pirate flag was Michel. Putting a political organizer on top of a journalistic enterprise not only broke the mold, it made maximum use of Michel's skills. The online platform she played a key role in building in 2004, Generation Dean, was central to making Vermont governor Howard Dean an early Democratic front-runner. Former associates thought it did even more; the project was called "the most successful campaign effort to organize young people since the McGovern campaign" in a book by University of Vermont sociology professor Thomas Streeter and Zephyr Teachout, a Duke law professor who worked as a Dean director.

Michel had joined the Dean effort while working at a

Vermont burrito shop. She expected to stuff envelopes, but she ended up researching the online campaigns of the 2000 presidential election and was soon tasked with recruiting young people over the Internet. It was a fast education for a Web publishing novice; before she knew it, Michel was customizing the open-source publishing package Drupal, sending mass e-mails and juggling a website, a blog, online calendars, and various political organizing databases. Under Michel's guidance, Generation Dean cultivated student organizers, set up a website where people could start or join a local chapter, circulated petitions, distributed e-postcards, and collected donations over the Web. It assembled niche groups like Punks for Dean and Young Professionals for Dean. Generation Dean even launched a six-state road tour that drew coverage from the *Daily Show* and scores of large daily newspapers. Although she had begun with only a donated computer whose monitor kept going blank and had only sporadic access to a lone volunteer programmer, Michel was central in creating a vaunted recruiting, organizing, and fund-raising machine.

The work of Off the Bus turned out to be remarkably similar. "It's signing up people for a campaign," Rosen told me, "but instead of trying to win the election for your candidate, you're trying to win the coverage, with outside-in journalism."

One of Off the Bus's best-performing projects fused the worlds of politics and journalism to a controversial extent. Michel devised the Grassroots Correspondents initiative as a way to get more volunteers writing and as a way to generate articles with a more personal voice. The project asked campaign activists to submit weekly journals reflecting briefly on something that happened in the course of their work. The only requirement was to be honest—and to write informally. Combining accounts from several correspondents, the project was the first to report that the Obama campaign was instructing female canvassers to try to get around McCain-supporting husbands in the homes they visited and speak directly to the wives—by sneaking around to the back door, for example, or by visiting the front door over and over again until they got the lady of the house. It was the sort of firsthand, insider account that a reader wouldn't find anywhere else.

The biggest star among the Grassroots Correspondents was Mayhill Fowler, a sixty-year-old Oakland, California, Democrat and novelist who jumped into Off the Bus with both feet, stalking the official Hillary Clinton and Barack Obama campaign buses in rental cars and with a $15 Sony voice recorder she bought on Amazon.com (it's now in the Newseum in Washington, D.C.). Fowler's work made it onto the front of the *New York Times* after she got former president Bill Clinton to vent to her on the campaign trail about a *Vanity Fair* writer who had questioned his judgment and associates; Clinton called the writer "sleazy," "slimy," and "dishonest," stirring up a national controversy over his emotional state as his wife, Hillary, lost ground to Barack Obama. Fowler filed scores of more substantive scoops, too, including an early warning that health care was replacing Iraq as the central campaign issue, according to information collected in a national canvas by the Obama campaign.

But none of that beat Bittergate. It's impossible to talk about Off the Bus without talking about Bittergate. It was Fowler's biggest story, the Grassroots Correspondents' biggest story, Off the Bus's biggest story, and, in the 2008 election, HuffPo's biggest story.

Fowler broke Bittergate in a way that would have been impossible for a traditional reporter: by leveraging her donations to and close relationships within the Obama campaign to secure an invitation to a San Francisco fund-raiser. There she recorded Obama's comments on "bitter" conservative voters from rural areas. Her scoop was one of the biggest news stories of the 2008 race, and took off in large part because it was such a break from form.

"Fowler's contribution was significant because it showed that Jane Q. Citizen could make a real impact on the political conversation," *Los Angeles Times* media writer James Rainey told me. "Obama later said the 'bitter' comments were his most damaging slip of the campaign."

"Mayhill Fowler captured a couple of [unscripted] moments in the 2008 cycle precisely because she was not a standard-issue reporter and because she was willing and able to go places— most importantly a 'closed press' fund-raiser—where journalists from the big media were barred."

Fowler's Off the Bus experience began in June 2007, after she attended an international women's conference in Amman, Jordan, hosted by Queen Rania, and resolved to follow international and political news more closely. This led her to the Huffington Post's daily e-mail blast, which one day solicited readers to join Off the Bus in covering Barack Obama's "walk for change," a canvassing event set to occur on a single day in hundreds of neighborhoods across the country. Fowler hated politics—her grandmother succumbed to a politically motivated attempt at seduction and was thrown out of the house by her grandfather, the former mayor of Memphis—but was intrigued by Obama, who had impressed her with a speech in which he said, "Faith has a place in the public square," affirming closer ties between religion and government. "Literally, I said out loud to myself, 'Oh my God, this guy is the next president of the United States,'" Fowler told me.

Soon after signing up with Off the Bus, Fowler became a die-hard convert. She sold her car, asked her husband and father for donations, and hit the trail. From Iowa to South Carolina to Texas, Nevada, North Carolina, and beyond, Fowler went to press conferences, speeches, and fundraisers, often employing a bit of subterfuge to get into or out of the press pen, for example, by unhinging a fence. Her reports—with headlines like OBAMA FAILS TO CLOSE THE DEAL IN KNOXVILLE; FROM THE OBAMA GRASSROOTS: STUDENTS FIRE IT UP; and HILLARY'S "SOFTER SIDE OF SEARS" SUMMER WARDROBE—were written in a diaristic style and peppered with personal observations.

"She treated this as a full-time job," Michel said of Fowler. "She said to me, 'I took this job as my husband took up the law—he went to the office every day.'"

Fowler didn't just write about the campaign; she was also a prolific Obama donor, having contributed the legal maximum of $2,300 to the Illinois senator's campaign (along with $100 to Hillary Clinton and $500 to Republican and fellow Tennessean Fred Thompson). This plus the fact that Fowler had become "friendly acquaintances," in her words, with a member of the California Obama Finance Committee, allowed her to secure a last-minute invitation to a sold-out

April 2008 Obama fund-raiser in a private mansion in San Francisco's wealthiest neighborhood. This would prove a pivotal bit of access.

At the fund-raiser, Fowler captured on her voice recorder three big pieces of news. Two have been largely lost to history: that Obama took a trip to Pakistan while in college, and that he wouldn't necessarily look for a running mate with strong foreign policy experience, since "foreign policy is the area where I am probably *most* confident that I know more and understand the world better than Senator Clinton or Senator McCain."

Fowler's third, blockbuster exclusive would come to be known simply as Bittergate: Obama, in the midst of a competitive Pennsylvania primary battle against Hillary Clinton, told the well-to-do San Franciscans packed into the mansion's library that "beaten-down" blue-collar communities in Pennsylvania were "where we are gonna have to do the most work—places where people feel the most cynical about government. . . . It's not surprising that they get bitter and they cling to guns or religion or antipathy toward people who aren't like them." Fowler felt betrayed, and that Obama was a "fraud"; this was the candidate, after all, who had underlined the valid role of religion in public life. "Obama's approach in San Francisco was not the way to go about explaining different Americans to one another—much less binding us together," Fowler wrote in *Notes from a Clueless Journalist*, her memoir about the 2008 election.

Fowler originally planned to sit on the "bitter" comments. "I was going to give Barack Obama a pass," she wrote. "I thought it was tacky to keep working an event or incident down to the last bit." But Michel knew there was more on Fowler's recorder and she coaxed the Bittergate story out of her.

Getting the main Huffington Post on board was a whole other battle. "It's like six o'clock in the morning California time," Fowler told me, "and Amanda calls me, this great tension in her voice, strung out like piano wire. And she said, 'Nico Pitney wants to talk to you.' I have no idea who Nico Pitney is."

Pitney was in charge of the Huffington Post's regular politics page, and had worked previously as a liberal activist.

"So I'm standing in the bathroom," Fowler continued, "and suddenly there's this voice on the line: 'Who the fuck are you, and how do we know this is true?' So I said, 'Well, actually, ever since last fall, I tape every interview I do. So I have a tape.' I put my cell phone on top of the tape recorder and let them hear it."

The story ran on Friday, April 11, 2008. It was immediately explosive.

The Bittergate piece upset Huffington and her HuffPo co-founder, Ken Lerer, who had hosted an Obama fund-raiser at his home a year earlier, Fowler and Cooper said. "It was very clear to me that the general orientation of the Huffington Post was very pro-Obama at that point," Cooper told me. But "we never felt any direct or indirect pressure to ideologically toe any lines, in terms of Clinton or Obama or whatever. . . . [Arianna] certainly had veto power. And she never exercised it." Huffington was on David Geffen's yacht in Tahiti when the Bittergate story ran, on a Friday; it's never been clear, even among HuffPo staffers, what she would have done if she had been around.

Fowler's story was read more than one hundred thousand times on its first day of publication and dominated the next several news cycles. It skyrocketed to the top of the Drudge Report and was the centerpiece of that weekend's episode of *Meet the Press*. The *New York Times* covered both the story and the backstory—Fowler's reservations about writing it, the process of editing it, and the fallout among professional reporters who thought Fowler broke from the basic ethical ground rules of journalism. Fowler was also accused of recording Obama surreptitiously, though she vigorously denied this. There were other people at the fund-raiser visibly recording Obama with personal video cameras and cell phones, she said. Also, the Obama staffer who invited her to the event knew Fowler had written for Off the Bus about a previous fund-raiser she attended.

"It was one of the defining stories about Obama," Ben Smith, who covered the election for Politico.com, told me. But "she presented it in a way that was deliberately unintelligible. . . . She did everything she could to kind of damage her own story. In other words, not to let her readers make up their own minds about what they thought of it."

Fowler, in characteristic Off the Bus fashion, had delivered her scoop wrapped in a frank disclosure of her own feelings, including a digression into why she had hesitated to write the story in the first place.

Smith added: "If, in any other campaign, a rich lady had shown up at a fund-raiser and come out and told reporters, or played reporters a tape of what had happened, which is something that happens all the time, they would have been called 'a source.' And now they're called 'a reporter.'"

Fowler and her daughter, a Princeton graduate student who shared her mother's first and last name, began to receive death threats. Bloggers who supported Obama were furious.

Fowler didn't think the Huffington Post did enough to stand by her. Right alongside her blockbuster story, on the HuffPo front page, was a strongly worded dissenting opinion from another HuffPo writer. Additional counterpoints peppered the site, including the Off the Bus section. "This is why I hate citizen journalism, I hate that whole idea," Fowler told me. "If I had been a paid reporter and I had gone in for that job and I had gone into the HR office and signed all those papers, we would've had an explicit and implicit contract between employer and employee, and they would've had my back, and there wouldn't have been a piece, sitting next to mine, full of all sorts of things about me, and after I had worked so hard to get all those stories to Huffington Post."

In retrospect, it seems inevitable that Bittergate tested the limits of Fowler's relationship with HuffPo, of politicians' interactions with the press, and of new media's ties to old media. This is what success looks like in the world of side projects and 20 percent time: disruptive. When an experimental project goes supernova, there is sometimes anger, and there is often a single moment of inflection. For Off the Bus, the inflection point was Bittergate. As with any other 20 percent supernova, the volume of controversy among colleagues and other incumbents was actually a mark of success. Paul Buchheit was jeered by Googlers who didn't want the company in the e-mail business, and was ordered to stop working on AdSense. Caterina Fake lost 17 percent of her staff—and nearly lost a pivotal company vote—because she wanted to bet big on the future of social photo sharing. Similarly, established media and politicians were threatened by Bittergate. The story seemed to break the rules. It seemed unfair and vaguely dangerous. But the hue and cry only confirmed that Off the Bus was changing the game, just as it had set out to do.

Bittergate did not just expose fissures between Fowler and Off the Bus, or between Off the Bus and the Obama campaign, or between Off the Bus and mainstream media. It also exposed a deep divide between Off the Bus and its host company, the Huffington Post. It forced a reckoning of long-simmering tensions between the two organizations, tensions rooted in the gulf between traditional journalism, as practiced in the HuffPo newsroom, and citizen journalism, as practiced by Off the Bus. Which set of principles would endure at HuffPo? And what would happen to the other set of principles?

This is the sort of question every 20 percent project must eventually answer, or have answered for it. Some, like Flickr, take over the host company entirely. Others, like Gmail and the Bronx Academy of Science, soldier on indefinitely while changing the broader organization only slightly. Others shine bright only to fizzle out, never transitioning from experiment to institution.

Throughout Off the Bus's operation, there was tension between the citizen journalism project and the main HuffPo politics staff in Washington, D.C. The regular HuffPo team, who operated like a traditional if opinionated newsroom, tended to regard the experimental Off the Bus team with befuddlement and suspicion. Off the Bus editorial director Cooper, meanwhile, clashed with the HuffPo regulars, whom he saw as hopelessly compromised by the Obama campaign and by the "on the bus" conventional wisdom that prevailed among elite political journalists. Cooper complained frequently to his old friend Roy Sekoff, the Huffington Post's founding editor and Arianna Huffington's right hand.

"In general, it was a constant frustration for us," Cooper said. "The pieces were not put on the front page, or they were put beneath the fold, or they were put there for a very short time. They were rarely vigorously promoted. . . . A deeply reported story that was crowd-sourced, and might have real breaking news, was often overshadowed or pushed aside for [HuffPo staff reporter] Sam Stein's daily report from a conference call, which was thinly disguised campaign propaganda."

Betsy Morgan, for her part, said the Huffington Post's editors did "an extraordinarily good job of editorial selection," and that the publication benefited from "having competing groups . . . competing for attention."

One of the first fights between Off the Bus and the Huffington Post proper concerned technology. The conflict first surfaced during Off the Bus's ambitious, highly distributed coverage of the Iowa caucuses. It became a festering problem.

Michel and Cooper wanted to create a Web page dedicated to the Iowa coverage, but HuffPo tech was insistent that Off the Bus had to make do with a generic, automatically generated "tag" page, which looked more like a list of search results than anything crafted by an editor.

"We fought, and fought, and fought," Cooper said, "and, finally, at the last minute, against tremendous resistance from everybody, Roy [Sekoff] put his finger on the scale, finally, and tipped it to create what they now call a 'big news page,' of which the Huffington Post now has hundreds."

The big news page, in the end, delivered far more value to the Huffington Post proper than to Off the Bus, and therein lies a tactic for other side projects: Make the case for new resources by arguing the benefits for everyone.

Pleading the broader benefit didn't always work for Off the Bus. The project was largely unsuccessful at wringing resources from HuffPo, even though Off the Bus was having to copy and paste e-mails from thousands of volunteers into the HuffPo publishing system, since it lacked a content management facility into which contributors could directly type their articles. "Amanda came knocking on Paul Berry the CTO's door," Morgan told me, "saying, 'You know, I would really like these tools and this and this and this.' And Paul Berry was like, 'What, are you kidding me? I've got all these things in front of me. I've got a new CEO. We've got all these crazy goals. And you know your project . . . is not totally core to what we are doing.'" The Huffington Post had just thirty employees at the time, was handling massive traffic growth, and was trying to grow further, Morgan said.

"I was talking to Arianna to get this job," Tomasic told me, "and in the interview, she says, 'Try telling me some of your ideas.' I thought there should be a running blog, kind of like a project blog. . . . And Arianna said, 'Oh, that sounds great. I know you must have your own tech people that you can lean on.' I was kind of like, 'Wait, what? You know, coming to the Huffington Post, and I have to lean on my friends here, to build these things?' And then when I got on board, Amanda just told me, basically, 'Forget tech fixes or adjustments.' It seemed shocking to me. Why would you run a kind of skunkworks, bootstrapping project and not provide pretty discrete technical support for that?"

Michel made the most of the tools on hand. "A lot of what she had," Morgan said, "she was kind of cobbling together. I mean she was working—to the best of my knowledge—she was working most of that off of this big Excel spreadsheet."

As Michel's experience shows, side projects have to bend over backward to make do with what they have, even as they lobby for what they need.

Tomasic said, "One thing I'm proud of is the fact that we did such a good job with horse shit, horrible technology. . . . We had four or five e-mail accounts and that's how we managed these two thousand contributors. And it was just a nightmare. Like, just imagine your worst overflowing e-mail account times twenty!"

When Bittergate broke, seven months before Election Day, the editorial tensions that had been simmering between Off the Bus editors and HuffPo regulars exploded. The regulars worried that the unfolding story was confirming their worst fears about Off the Bus contributors: that they were sloppy and untrustworthy. The facts would prove this emphatically not the case, but the early days of the scandal were chaotic and HuffPo had limited faith in its side project. Michel and Cooper sensed this distrust and believed the HuffPo regulars were undermining their big moment, perhaps out of jealousy. Even if they weren't, who was HuffPo, with its staff of largely young and inexperienced D.C. editors, to condescend to Off the Bus's Cooper, who had worked as a journalist and author for thirty-five years, or Michel, who had been integrating politics and online publishing before HuffPo even existed?

The tensions exploded in a back-and-forth e-mail exchange, which began when Michel complained that the regular Huffington Post Politics section had only linked to, and not explicitly credited, Off the Bus for the Bittergate story. Politics editor Nico Pitney replied with a complaint that "virtually every aspect of the rollout of this piece was poorly handled," claiming he was caught unaware when Bittergate was actually published; saying the audio recording of Obama's remarks should have been published at the same time as the story, not later; and stating that the story "needlessly jeopardized our relationship with the Obama campaign . . . we could have done them the favor of alerting them that we were about to publish highly controversial remarks."

This, predictably, provoked an intense defense from Cooper and Michel, who called Pitney's e-mail an "outrageous note" (Cooper) that "offends me" (Michel). They pointed out it had taken them a full week to convince Fowler to write the story—"she showed up at the office and FIRST wanted to talk with me about getting paid for the audio and a job," Michel wrote—making coordination hard, though they kept Pitney briefed along the way. Furthermore, it had been a six-hour technological struggle to convert and embed the audio from Fowler's voice recorder. Finally, as Cooper put it, "we seriously weighed all of the ethical considerations attached to these pieces. . . . It is not our job to coordinate in any manner with political campaigns we report on. Period. . . . Never before has a single HuffPost political piece gotten so much attention and been so central to the entire debate. We should all be proud of this accomplishment and giving some props to the people who made it happen instead of blaming them for a 'botched' rollout."

Rosen and Huffington tried to quell the fight with a call for "high fives and congratulations all around," as Rosen put it. "Anything that goes wrong this time should be corrected for the next. I sense that whatever tensions there are in a fast-moving organization, everyone actually agrees on that."

Still, there was no denying that near the pinnacle of Off the Bus's achievements—"a direct fulfillment of a vision Arianna and I had when we talked about this project in the spring on 2007," as Rosen wrote—the project found itself most bitterly at odds with its host company. That did not bode well for the future.

Michel and Cooper's final reckoning with the Huffington Post proper came shortly before the election. There was no question about Off the Bus's future—Michel and Cooper wanted Off the Bus to end. Keeping the citizen journalism project outside HuffPo would prolong the infighting between Off the Bus staff and HuffPo regulars and extend the Off the Bus team's second-class status. Off the Bus was done experimenting. It had accumulated many hard-won lessons about what worked and what didn't in citizen journalism. It was time to spread those lessons to the rest of HuffPo.

Michel and Cooper had some hope of selling this integration to HuffPo executives. Cooper had known Huffington for ten years, and become close as well with Sekoff, her number-two editor. Cooper had helped Huffington with her 2000 "Shadow Conventions," bipartisan events to discuss issues sidelined at the official Democratic and Republican party conventions; with her 2003 gubernatorial campaign; as well as with the 2005 launch of the Huffington Post, where Cooper suggested, among other things, that Huffington make herself a more prominent part of the site. Upon hiring Cooper for Off the Bus, "Arianna said to me, 'Marc, this will be like old times,'" Cooper said.

The integration model Michel and Cooper proposed was more like a takeover. Their plan, outlined in a lengthy e-mail memo, was to clear Pitney and the rest of the existing political journalism staff from their positions of power.

"We take Off the Bus and we make it the Huffington Post," Cooper said, summarizing the memo. "We consolidate this into one reporting apparatus. We get some real editors involved . . . I suggested we needed eight or ten real editors.

"We break down all the silos and all the firewalls. We get rid of the six categories [of Huffington Post content, listed at the top of the home page]. We have a big [unified] pot of money. And some people will be paid freelance, or a daily fee. . . . We'd probably fire the current reporters, but we'd probably hire four or five reporters.

"We would use a pro-am model; our reporters and editors would lead our readers in investigative and news projects. Which is exactly what we should have done, and Roy loved it, endorsed it, took it to a meeting in New York. . . . Arianna loved the idea and said, 'Absolutely this is the way we are going to go. Marc is absolutely correct. Everybody is right. The only objection I have is that we're not going to remove Nico and all these other people from the team.'

"And we said, 'But we can't do it. How can we do it? You want us to do it, but you're going to let this group of six people retain power over everything?' And Arianna said, 'Well, I'm not going to fire any of them.'"

At the end of Michel and Cooper's final reckoning, it looked like Off the Bus would be one of those 20 percent–style projects that shine bright and fizzle out. Cooper and Michel left the Huffington Post just after the election; Nico Pitney, who had asked Off the Bus's most vaunted contributor "Who the fuck are you?" was promoted to executive editor within two years of the election. HuffPo let Off the Bus sit dormant for months after the election. Huffington's godson, the heir to a computer fortune, took it over. Fowler was thrown in the same editing pool as the thousands of other unpaid HuffPo bloggers after the election, and she publicly announced in September 2010 that she would no longer write for the site. "It wasn't just the pay," Fowler told me of her decision to quit. "I've been sending them pieces, I never hear back. . . . At the end of the day you just need some editorial support."

6

How a Top Chef Started Over

Thomas Keller's Ad Hoc Brought 20
Percent Time into Haute Cuisine

By 2006, Thomas Keller was riding high. His new restaurant in New York, Per Se, had just received three Michelin stars. His flagship restaurant in Yountville, California, The French Laundry, was revered as the best restaurant in the country, maybe the world. His thriving chain of French bistros, Bouchon, had spread from Napa Valley to Las Vegas. But something was missing amid the jammed reservation lines, five hundred–plus employees, and high-tech videoconferencing screens that linked his New York and Napa Valley kitchens.

Keller looked back fondly to his more obscure days. When The French Laundry first opened in 1994, for example, there was barely enough money for a fresh coat of paint and some scraps of carpet; the chairs were donated, the silverware secondhand, and the restaurant made do without a single sauté pan ("we sautéed in pots," Keller later said). That was before the kitchen quadrupled in size in the first of several pricey renovations, before The French Laundry started opening seven days a week and for lunch on weekends to boost revenue, before the expansion restaurants—back when every single person on Keller's staff worked the same shifts together, drank wine after work together, and shared the same days off, often enjoying a softball game. Keller wanted some of that camaraderie back. He was ready for something new and at the same time ready for something very old. "I wanted to have a small staff that worked together and had a real bonding experience with one another," Keller told me, "a throwback to the days when a five-day-per-week restaurant was normal. . . . Kind of like The French Laundry when I first bought it."

Keller's nostalgia would soon lead to the launch of a new restaurant, Ad Hoc. Intended to be a temporary side project, it flowered quickly and profitably into a mecca for California foodies and savvy wine-country tourists. Later, it became a franchise, with a line of products at Williams-Sonoma, a cookbook that sold 235,000 copies and went into twelve printings, and an eye toward expanding to other cities. "It's been hugely successful," *San Francisco Chronicle* food editor Michael Bauer told me. Keller didn't do it alone or by fiat. Ad Hoc, as you'll see, developed organically over many conversations with staff. But there's no question the restaurant was catalyzed by Keller's passion to make something that reset what restaurants had become in America—and in his own company.

For Keller, his business, and his culinary brain trust, Ad Hoc was very much a side project, conceived and built in everyone's spare time. Keller worked as executive chef at two other restaurants throughout the launch and after. Ad Hoc did eventually have a full-time chef de cuisine and staff, but none expected their jobs there to be permanent; Ad Hoc was supposed to close a few months after it opened its doors.

One key takeaway from Keller's Ad Hoc experience, for other 20 percent time projects, is the importance of using constraints, especially time and financial constraints, to bust through perfectionism. Because Ad Hoc was intended to live a short time, Keller simply had to let go of certain details, no easy feat for such a famously obsessive chef. In this way, Ad Hoc had something in common with tech projects like Flickr and the hacks at Yahoo! Hack Day, which were similarly energized by tight deadlines.

Ad Hoc also has a lesson to teach about the importance of finding a way to make a project emotionally resonant. Just as Huffington Post's Off the Bus succeeded thanks to the emotional investments of its volunteer contributors, Ad Hoc came into being to feed the emotional hunger of Keller and his team. Hearkening back to childhood food memories and touching on fondness for family and staff camaraderie helped Keller fire up his employees. Ad Hoc succeeded in the marketplace, meanwhile, by resonating emotionally with customers. Keller and his team selected dishes by identifying "reference points" in customers' lives that dishes would touch on.

The saga of Ad Hoc began with the end of a sunny Yountville restaurant called Wine Garden, which served small plates and wines from the Napa Valley vintner family that owned it. It failed to drum up enough business and closed in January 2006 after sixteen months of operation. Keller smelled an opportunity. His French Laundry was just half a mile up the road, and his Bouchon just four blocks away. The property on which the Wine Garden sat was large enough to accommodate some affordable housing Keller had to build for an inn he was developing. One thing led to another, and Keller found himself with a new piece of land, a new mortgage to pay, and a dormant eatery. The chef has always maintained that he bought Wine Garden primarily as a site for housing, but the first thing he did—and indeed the first project on which he unleashed his considerable enthusiasm—was to remake that empty restaurant.

The restaurant became the lab where Keller experimented with his dreams for a "throwback" establishment. Eventually, Keller wanted the space to house a restaurant pairing hamburgers and half bottles of wine, a concept he'd been kicking around in one form or another for sixteen years. Keller knew he would call this restaurant Burgers and Bottles, but the culinary specifics were up in the air. They had to end up dazzling, because by 2006, the idea of a high-end burger joint was old hat. Daniel Boulud, Danny Meyer, and Hubert Keller had each done one already. Keller and his culinary director, Jeffrey Cerciello, tried some ambitious burger experiments—"a lot of things with sous-vide," Cerciello told me—and didn't find anything that worked.

So Keller decided to open a temporary restaurant for a few months while he refined Bottles and Burgers a bit more. The Wine Garden would become a blank canvas, a low-risk playground for new ideas. Keller could hardly have been more thrilled. One night after dinner at The French Laundry, when all the customers had gone home, he peppered his crew with questions about what to do. "I said, 'Guys, what would you do if you had a restaurant to open?'" Keller told one interviewer. "And we threw it around the table." Keller wrote up the results of their brainstorm in an e-mail to his executives at Thomas Keller Restaurant Group. Subject line: "A fun idea!"

What if we did a temporary restaurant at the Wine Garden? FUN, Simple, Affordable, 1 Service, No Menu, 4–5 nights a week. Maybe supper on Sunday.

Here it is! Ad Hoc. Opening as soon we can. Wed–Sun. . . .

NO MENU. 4 courses, salad course served family style, Protein (roast, slice, and serve), Starch and vegetable. Old style, SIMPLE. . . .

Staff = 1 manager type, 1 wine guy, 1 chef type (maybe me), servers, cooks, and porters. May be a good way to utilize our Bouchon private dining staff. 60 covers a night, 75.00 check average, What do you think???? Let me know, T

Keller's underlings thought the e-mail was a joke. It was sent on April Fools' Day, after all, and the "FUN" restaurant Keller described seemed out of character, to say the least. "My response was, 'Thomas doesn't do fun. Thomas does complicated,'" Cerciello said.

But Keller was serious, and with help from Cerciello and Bouchon's executive sous-chef Dave Cruz, he expanded his initial e-mail into a fuller plan for the temporary restaurant.

Ad Hoc was designed from the get-go to be low maintenance. The team needed to operate such that there would be time to research their burger concept, time for Cerciello to keep working as executive chef at Bouchon, and time for Keller to do likewise at Per Se and The French Laundry. Only dinner would be served, and diners would have no food choices, being served a four-course set menu. The place was open only Wednesday through Sunday, not six or seven days per week, like Keller's other restaurants. No reservations would be accepted. The food would always cost the same, $45. Diners would pour their own wine and dole out their own portions from large "family style" bowls and platters.

The service was stripped down, but at the same time it added something to the mood. "It's meant to be like you're at home," Keller told me. "And you put the wine on the table and, yeah, you grab it, but you serve the person next to you and you pass it around. Same thing with the water, the food. . . . It's a point of social engagement."

Taking the theme of low-maintenance simplicity further, Keller's team also constrained the kitchen. Staff aimed to create entrées that could be prepared entirely in a single pot. Keller may have built his reputation serving elaborate meals prepared in a grand, institutional French style, but he always yearned to re-create the comfort foods of his childhood. Even the lusciously complicated dishes at his luxury restaurants tended to be intricate descendants of childhood favorites like macaroni and cheese and peanut butter and jelly. At Ad Hoc, he and Cerciello worked to create a dining experience even closer to their roots. Cruz later said that when he wasn't sure how to handle a particular dish, he would just ask himself how he would do it at home. The restaurant's approach was also inspired by the food Keller's restaurant workers prepared for one another between shifts, "family meals" created ad hoc, built from whatever ingredients were handy.

"It gave me the opportunity to say, 'Okay, now I get to break away from the French and start to introduce a lot of things from California,'" Cerciello said, "things from North Africa, things from Spain, from Italy, and to create these wonderful robust dishes . . . I knew that I wanted to serve them in big vessels that were just really saucy and hardy. . . . Big bowls of salads or braised meats—the whole idea of sitting around the table, having a conversation—that was important."

Keller and Cerciello crafted a dining room and kitchen that, like Ad Hoc's food, were simple, robust, and influenced by the distant past. They left the fully equipped Wine Garden kitchen largely as it was. Cerciello just installed some rails, changed the orientation, and made it a little more open. The staff did without heating and air-conditioning in the production areas, no small feat in the California summer. Knowing that the restaurant was temporary helped Cerciello resist his urge to open up the bar and reorient it to face the kitchen.

In the dining room, Keller's team just applied a clean coat of paint and furnished with secondhand items bought at a consignment store. Their butcher's block was an antique Keller had lying around at home; the maître d' stand was pulled out of storage, having been discarded from The French Laundry; and Cerciello picked up additional items at an antiques store and at a secondhand San Francisco shop named Cookin', famous for its surly service and "dusty," "dirty" and "precarious" piles of esoteric kitchen supplies, as described on

Yelp.com. The bare-bones approach to Ad Hoc's interior was very much like the Spartan opening of The French Laundry (Cruz, at least, had sauté pans).

Keller's spare approach to building out Ad Hoc helped reduce risk. In the end, his team spent less than a quarter of the cost of a typical Thomas Keller Restaurant Group launch, according to Cerciello, who recently opened his own restaurant, Farm Shop, in Los Angeles. "This was nothing," he said. "We just made the best of what we had because there really wasn't a big budget for it."

The ethic of thrifty reuse at Ad Hoc mirrored the way Gmail, AdSense, and Flickr were launched by slightly adapting old code (a discussion search engine, a porn filter, and a video game chat system, respectively). Reusing old tools is a useful way to satisfy the 20 Percent Doctrine tenet of launching a prototype as quickly as possible, as Keller has discovered. "Someone like Thomas [Keller] . . . how many times has he assembled the basic framework of putting together a food establishment?" I was asked by Daniel Raffel, who worked as a cook under Keller at Per Se and who as a programmer has run Hack Days for TechCrunch and others. "Enough that now the pieces are familiar to him. . . . He knows what things are necessary, and what things are unnecessary, and where to invest time, and where to cut back, and he can basically slap stuff together super quickly."

"Ad Hoc really is a good example of a hack in the sense that in the software developer world somebody who is a Rails [Web framework] developer would probably be like, 'Okay, I'm going to use [pre-written framework software] like Heroku, and Rails 3.0, and Sinatra.' That's equivalent to

[Keller] finding the real estate agent who is going to find the space, finding the manager who is going to run the restaurant, figuring out what point-of-sale software to use, figuring out what pots and pans you're going to use, what the vendors are going to be for your produce. Once you've got the basic framework, if you have any original ideas and you're actually passionate about what you do, you should be able to do something interesting with those ingredients."

The benefits of reuse notwithstanding, a frugal temporary restaurant wasn't an easy sell to Keller's august culinary crew. Cruz initially refused to leave his perch as the executive sous-chef at Keller's upscale Bouchon to become chef de cuisine at a casual, short-lived new restaurant. "They had put up these memos about the concept of Ad Hoc," Cruz told me. "And, honestly, it had on there that it would be food that Thomas grew up with. For example, fried chicken, beef Stroganoff, meat loaf, you know, spaghetti and meatballs. As the executive sous-chef at Bouchon, I had a staff of probably around eighteen to twenty cooks, and a full staff of porters I was in charge of. . . . I just kind of wanted to stick with fine food." Or, as Cruz put it in the Ad Hoc cookbook, "I didn't want to leave my post at an elegant restaurant serving French classics to go make 'family meals.'" But Cruz was pressed into service for the first two months of the launch, anyway ("it was decided unilaterally," he wrote). And one day he was flipping through the French Laundry cookbook, looking for menu ideas, and had an epiphany. He came across an essay Keller had written on the importance of the "family meal," and how preparing food for one's coworkers in a passionate and caring way was a fundamental first step on the road to being a great chef. "Right then the whole picture became clear for me—this was what cooking was all about," he wrote.

After five months' preparation, Ad Hoc opened in September 2006. It was a quick hit. Waits for tables grew well beyond forty-five minutes, forcing the restaurant to begin accepting reservations. The bar was regularly packed. In an effort to temper the crush of phone calls, Ad Hoc began disclosing its menu in advance, initially via voice mail robocalls. Ad Hoc has had to add seats to meet demand. After expanding to 94 from 70 chairs, it now averages 150 covers a night, and sometimes over 200. As stated in Keller's original e-mail to staff, he had hoped for just 60 covers per night.

Some of the early popularity can be chalked up to Keller's sterling reputation. And food bloggers and local newspapers also helped stoke interest. But above all, customers were responding to the food. "It has food that resonates with people—they've all had it before," Keller said. "Whether it's barbecue or whether it's fried chicken, whether it's skirt steak, all the different things that we serve resonate with people because it's something that they have reference points for. I think that's what Ad Hoc is about, those reference points."

All the top people on Keller's team brought up these "reference points," either specifically or in the general idea that the food at Ad Hoc evoked something warm and comfortable, like Keller's staff "family meals," or dinners people ate during childhood, or just the communal nature of breaking bread as a group. "Finally," I thought, "an explanation for how I felt when *I* dined at Ad Hoc." Whether with my wife, with another couple, or with my mom and brother, an Ad Hoc dinner always seemed to be a bonding experience, a glowing mélange of food and camaraderie at the end of a long day in wine country. Eating at The French Laundry with five friends had, in contrast, been revelatory, a meal to end all meals, an epic four-hour culinary enlightenment—but not the time of friendship I experienced at Ad Hoc.

Few people in any field have the skills or resources to create a product as perfect as the dining experience at The French Laundry. But as Ad Hoc shows, you can amplify the resources available to you and mitigate the effects of a tight deadline by creating something that touches people's emotions. Ad Hoc's reference points affected customers and staff alike. Making something with emotional appeal can likewise help you drum up support, recruit helpers, and delight your customers. As we saw in chapter 5, Off the Bus attracted and retained contributors by creating an emotionally rewarding experience for their volunteers. It similarly attracted readers with stories that felt authentic and that packed emotional punch, like Bittergate. Joan Sullivan, meanwhile, spent perhaps as much effort preparing her high school students for college psychologically as she did preparing them academically, as we saw in chapter 4. She insisted on uniforms, sent students on college tours and cultural expeditions, and relentlessly ratcheted up students' expectations of themselves. Feelings count, and connecting with people's humanity will take a side project a long way, even if your project involves exactingly efficient computer software, precisely calculated profit strategies, or intricately prepared cuisine.

Beyond the emotional appeal of the food at Ad Hoc was its quality; Keller obsessed over his temporary restaurant like it was one of his premium-priced flagships. While dishes like fried chicken and beef Stroganoff give the impression of simplicity, their preparation in the Ad Hoc kitchen is a complex undertaking. As Cruz put it, "We want to take whatever techniques we know, whatever experience or technology we have, to something that's familiar, and refine it, and refine it." So the short ribs weren't just braised, they were cooked sous-vide style for forty-eight hours, then seared, roasted, and served atop lentils, bacon, and herbs. The fried chicken wasn't just battered with buttermilk and spices, it was brined for six hours beforehand. The meat loaf was made from ultra-tender Wagyu beef and served with garlic-crushed potatoes. Accompaniments might include olive oil–poached mushrooms or slow-baked piquillo peppers. One *Wall Street Journal* writer retitled Ad Hoc's chicken soup "impossible soup" after wrestling with the complex cookbook recipe for three hours. But putting extreme effort into seemingly casual food is what made Ad Hoc work so well.

"Emotionally simple food is not a simple task," high-end restaurant consultant Clark Wolf told me. "Frankly, I am much more inclined, and most diners are much more inclined, to want something that is simple emotionally. And the problem is we mistake the emotionally simple for technically simple."

Keller is a perfectionist, and was as fastidious in assembling an interim business as when building something permanent. He did not reduce the quality of his work. But he did narrow his scope, and that's another reason Ad Hoc was a hit. The way he winnowed down a gourmet restaurant to its barest essentials worked a sort of magic: Ad Hoc offered Keller's usual transcendental culinary brilliance at a fraction of the usual cost, $45 versus $210 at The French Laundry. It also applied his culinary technique to a new class of dishes, casting old comfort foods in a new light and bringing his cooking to a wider base of customers.

"It was fortuitous for him because he is such a perfectionist," Bauer said. "If he was opening Ad Hoc permanently, he may have done too much. And the way it was, he did what he could, as perfectly as he could, in this short amount of time, without spending money. Because he was kind of restrained, it kind of made it more casual, and I think, that probably made it more appealing."

"He makes a good point," Keller said of Bauer's remarks. "As a temporary restaurant the finances we spent on it and the commitments we made were minimal compared to when we did The French Laundry or now today when we do Bouchon or Per Se."

We've seen with Hack Day, Flickr, and now Ad Hoc how deadlines and other constraints act as forcing mechanisms that spark cracklingly intense creative output. Yet it's still eye-opening to learn that the same mechanism works entirely outside the tech world, among the top-flight chefs in Thomas Keller Restaurant Group. Keller is probably not someone who would identify himself with the "worse is better" tenet of the 20 Percent Doctrine we identified in the introduction. And yet there's no question that being forced to let go a little led to big wins at Ad Hoc.

"Steve Jobs would say, 'real artists ship,' " Raffel, the chef and hacker, told me. "For [Keller] to be able to put this thing into the world that was as rough as that place was, it's a major accomplishment. He's someone who just like refines and refines and refines, and so for him the ultimate hack was that he launched this thing that was such a radical departure.

"To limit the amount of time you give yourself to create new things, you have to play by a new set of rules. To me that's what Ad Hoc represented. It was this big pitch shift, and [Keller] putting a lot of constraints on himself. . . . You can't really fail if you set up the boundary that you're only doing this for six months."

If Keller can find corners he's comfortable cutting in a pinch, you can, too. The best way to find those shortcuts is by using a forcing mechanism like the ones Keller used. Embrace small budgets, embrace tight deadlines, and embrace the idea that what you make today will soon be undone, either because it's temporary or because it will be iteratively improved into something unrecognizably better.

The elemental, emotionally resonant food, the communal dishes, the spare dining room, the lower prices—all this made Ad Hoc feel more like a family gathering place and less like a fancy restaurant, further heightening its appeal. Ad Hoc's happy, tightly bonded staff fed into the family feel, as well. Since the restaurant is only open five days per week, the same crew is always together and has the same days off. Most have been there for two years or more. Keller and his team scheduled start times, end times, and breaks to keep the staff comfortable, well rested, and together. "I think that translated into a really comfortable environment, and passed on to the guests that sat down in our chairs," Cruz said.

In November 2006, before Ad Hoc went permanent, Bauer reviewed it in the *Chronicle*. Keller was worried. "You aren't going to review a temporary restaurant, are you?" he asked. He needn't have fretted. Ad Hoc got three and a half stars out of four. "Ad Hoc seems fully realized," Bauer wrote. "I don't think it's in Keller's genes to do anything halfway, temporary or not." That was true. As Keller put it, "We can't diminish standards just because it's a different format, a different concept, or a different price."

When Bauer's review was published, Ad Hoc was still officially "temporary." But all the positive chatter from diners and critics stoked gossip that Ad Hoc would go permanent. "People would come up to me in the street and say, 'You have to keep it open,'" Cruz said. Keller and Cerciello recounted similar stories. By the time January rolled around, Ad Hoc did not close as scheduled. Instead, Keller and Cerciello announced Ad Hoc would continue indefinitely and that the Burgers and Bottles was on hold.

"That was the thing," Cerciello told me. "After six months, we said, 'Here we are. We created a new brand, whether we like it or not.' It was a great opportunity. I mean we could do these in Los Angeles [or] in Las Vegas."

Keller said that he'd "love to" create additional Ad Hocs and "hopefully" eventually will, if all the restaurant's oddities prove workable outside of Napa Valley and the San Francisco area. In the meantime, he's already followed up Ad Hoc with Addendum, a take-out shack behind Ad Hoc, offering a box lunch three days a week. And he's launched an additional temporary concept in the form of a French Laundry "pop-up" restaurant, which served a $400 nine-course lunch and dinner inside Harrods department store in London for ten days. If Ad Hoc was Keller's version of a 20 percent project, then the pop-up was his version of a hack day.

"I don't think his passion is maintaining things, I think his passion is creating things," Raffel said. "And then seeing how many of them he can keep in the air at the same time. At this point he's clearly like a master juggler."

At Ad Hoc, Keller not only learned how to shorten his creation cycle, he did it in a way that preserved that sense of magic that suffused his other endeavors. "It's had an enormous influence," Clark Wolf said of Ad Hoc. "It's given people confidence that something straightforward and emotionally simple can be appealing in the business. You know, I think that it's the best kind of mom-and-pop. . . . The fact is, it is kind of an American secret that really successful people who are actually already successful—not on their way, but already successful—like to eat comforting, well-made, what we sometimes think of as 'low' food. You know, if you don't have anything to prove, eat something simple and wonderful."

CONCLUSION

I started this book by suggesting that American business is being remade from the bottom up. We're seeing the early flowerings of a movement toward more creative freedom in corporate workplaces, toward systems that encourage employee self-determination, and toward teams that are valued for the speed and distinctiveness of their output rather than for its sheer scale. This movement has revived old ideas about harvesting innovation from the margins of large organizations, and placed those ideas in a modern context of high-speed networks, new communication tools, digital goods, and global distribution networks.

It started, logically enough, at Google, the nexus of networked innovation, where bleeding-edge Internet tools, surplus wealth, and a rich Silicon Valley tradition of tinkering combined to produce 20 percent time. Twenty percent time's underlying principles are spreading and becoming more broadly useful, adapting to organizations with less wealth, less history, and less agility, and to people without 20 percent–friendly employers, but with the ardor to join a passion project outside the workplace.

We saw the core tenets behind 20 percent time, aka the 20 Percent Doctrine, at work as we toured through six case studies in the preceding chapters. Some were set in the tech companies of Silicon Valley, others in Wine Country restaurant kitchens, some on the campaign trail, others in Bronx classrooms. Each found its own sort of success.

But for all of their individuality, these different projects had a lot in common. Certain lessons popped up repeatedly, sometimes in wildly different contexts. I said at the beginning of this book that I wanted to give you a fighting chance at turning your side project into a successful virtual startup inside your company. With an eye toward that goal, I've highlighted some key lessons within the individual cases, but it might also be useful to recap those lessons in a different format.

A side project unfolds in stages. Here are some things we've learned in the preceding chapters about what to do in each of those stages.

EARLY STAGE—BUILDING IDENTITY

In the early stage of a side project, you're inspired by a new idea, evaluate that idea, refine it, and begin work. Your experiments are frenzied, your potential seems limitless, and your idea is highly vulnerable to dying as a result of fear, boredom, and neglect.

- **Scratch your own itch.** Thomas Keller was inspired to build Ad Hoc because he wanted to relive the old days, when, as he put it, "you work five days a week with the same people every day and you take the same days off. Those restaurants are far and few between these days." Jay Rosen launched Off the Bus with Arianna Huffington because he was hungry to improve news coverage after decades of observing how it failed consumers. And Paul Buchheit built Gmail because, as far as he was concerned, e-mail was still broken years after he'd toyed in college with the idea of fixing it.

  All these people were building for themselves. Similarly, you should be your own first customer. Make something you really want for yourself. Do it to eliminate something that annoys the hell out of you, or to create something in an area where you feel inspired. The hunger to scratch your own itch is the bedrock on which a passion project is built.

- **Be conspicuously different, even defiant.** You've got to be visibly different, as both a product and a team. It doesn't hurt to be outright rebellious sometimes. You need a bold message and distinctive identity. It is incredibly hard even for a full-time company like a start-up to break through the wall of noise that is today's marketplace, to get attention, and to lodge in people's minds. It's even harder when you're working in your spare time inside a company with different priorities.

The desire for distinctiveness is why the Huffington Post's Off the Bus shunned news stories that sounded too professional, created a Special Ops team, and launched brands like Grassroots Correspondents and Eyes and Ears that had no equivalent whatsoever in the mainstream media. Yahoo! Hack Day likewise took off because Chad Dickerson pushed the hackathon format into bold, highly visible new territory with the alt-rock concert, oddball hacks, and wafting pot smoke of Open Hack Day, because of his unauthorized press leaks, and because he embraced subversive hacks like "Who's the Boss?" Joan Sullivan put her students in the Bronx in uniforms and took them to museums, cultural monuments, and college campuses that showed them in a very concrete way that they were a special cadre of students. And of course Gmail was possible, thanks only to Paul Buchheit's brutally—distinctively!—rough first prototype.

- **Connect with people emotionally.** You are not just delivering a product, you are creating an experience. Your passion project lights you up inside, and it should do the same for both your customers and your coworkers. You want to create something emotionally resonant, a product that delights people, even the people building it. Even before you know exactly what your product will be, your own high expectations will create an experience for those around you. As Sullivan said, "You do need to believe that [your goal] is possible, because people's intuition . . .

their sense that this is a credible belief . . . is strong, generally, [on] your team."

If you can learn this lesson and create something that touches people's feelings, you will have at your disposal a powerful lever that can multiply the impact of whatever resources and expertise you invest in your project. Thomas Keller credits the runaway success of Ad Hoc as both a restaurant and a cookbook not only to the quality of the food but to the fact that the restaurant touched people's "reference points," with family-style dining and dishes like fried chicken, ribs, fish and chips, and roasted sirloin that took people back to their childhoods. Flickr, similarly, took off after its tagging feature turned photo uploading into an emotionally powerful social experience. And of course Off the Bus succeeded where prior journalism efforts had failed because it tried doggedly to create a positive experience for its thousands of contributors and to make human, relatable political coverage for its many readers.

- **Build something simple and quick.** *Make a simple prototype, quickly.* If there is one lesson that is ubiquitous among successful 20 percent projects, it's this one. Version 1 of Gmail was built in a few hours and could only read one guy's e-mail. AdSense was prototyped overnight. Version 1 of Flickr was built in just over two months. Hack days succeed by making people build something in twenty-four hours or less.

The rough prototype is also a staple of non-software products. Ad Hoc was built in a four-month sprint for less than a quarter of the cost of Thomas Keller's other restaurants. The proposal for the Bronx Academy of Letters was written in two weeks while Sullivan was teaching full-time. And Off the Bus came together, as Amanda Michel put it, after "Arianna [Huffington] had a conversation with Jay [Rosen], and they made a very fast decision."

• **Broke and sweating is your happy place.** Constraints are your friends. Embrace tight deadlines and a dearth of resources. Seemingly impossible timelines help you whittle down your idea to its most potent essence and get something out the door, while constrained resources force you to abandon bad ideas and encourage you to seek out novel solutions to problems rather than buying common ones. Flickr was born not just from some spare-time hacking but also from the death throes of a video game company. Ad Hoc came about because Keller, a famous perfectionist, told himself he was going to throw away the restaurant, and so shouldn't spend too much money launching it or take too much time planning it. Google Reader launched because of a one-month ultimatum. Hack days are built on the power of deadlines. And tough conditions in the New York City schools and in the Bronx pushed Sullivan to create a pioneering endowment for her public high school.

MIDDLE STAGE—FIGHTING FOR SUPPORT

In the middle stage of a 20 percent–style project, other people become involved. You are trying to attract customers or users, as well as teammates and allies. You improve the product.

- **Iterate fast.** You want to improve incrementally and release a steady stream of new versions. The key is to keep each iteration small and manageable. This style of product development has a number of advantages. More improved versions mean more opportunities to get feedback on your product from testers, colleagues, and early customers. This reduces the risk of wasting a lot of time developing in the wrong direction or that you'll be surprised at how people react to your improvements. Keeping your versions small also helps you more quickly determine how much work is involved with each improvement and how long each one will take. In addition, more iterations mean more excuses to talk about your project and more opportunities for other people to spread the word, raising the profile of the project.

  Gmail is the poster child for iteration, having incrementally improved over the course of two and a half years from the point where it was described, in Googler Chris Wetherell's words, as "the worst thing ever" to the point where it became the fastest-growing e-mail service on the planet. Flickr, too, evolved via baby steps, gradually transforming from an instant messenger application to a photo website to a full-blown social network. Innovation benefits from iteration outside of tech, too. Sullivan's high school started with just ninth grade and added a grade a year for four years. At that point, it began adding a middle school. "You didn't have to staff up all grades all at once," former New York City schools chancellor Joel Klein told me. "You could kind of staff up the ninth grade, the tenth and eleventh, and then twelfth, staff up the seventh grade, basically building a culture that was aligned with your thinking."

- **Decide what to measure, and set a benchmark goal.** To decide how to develop Gmail, Buchheit set a goal of accumulating one hundred happy users inside Google. He later said, basically, that once he got to one hundred users, getting to millions was not much harder. "One hundred doesn't sound like a lot," Buchheit said, "but it turns out people are pretty similar to each other, so if you can make one hundred people happy, usually you can make more." At Ad Hoc, Keller set a goal at the outset of doing about sixty "covers," or customers, per night. At Flickr, Caterina Fake's main statistic was the bank balance of Ludicorp, which was perpetually in danger of going under. But she had another benchmark she watched, total user sign-ups per day; she knew Flickr was in danger when it briefly dropped below ten.

It's great that you are passionate enough about something to launch a side project in your spare time. But you cannot be guided by emotions alone. You need an objective yardstick with which you will measure your project's progress, and you should set a goal that can be measured with this yardstick. Try not to get lost in or obsessed with statistics, but do have some numbers to keep you grounded.

- **Be needy.** The best way to enlist people as allies is to show them concrete things they can personally do to improve your project. Wetherell showed the source code for a prototype version of Google Reader to a smarter programmer, knowing the programmer would wince at the low quality of Wetherell's code and be tempted to rewrite it himself. It worked. Also at Google, Buchheit's AdSense prototype was crude, just as his Gmail prototype had been. Google assigned a whole new team to AdSense, which completely remade the product and launched it in time to fund Gmail. "An extremely talented team was formed to build the project, and within maybe six months a live beta was launched," Buchheit later wrote. At Off the Bus, meanwhile, Michel successfully recruited citizen journalists by showing them how their professional expertise, their geographic location, or their political background made them especially valuable to the Huffington Post's political coverage.

- **Be confident.** While you want to make clear to people how you need help, at the same time you also need to show zealous confidence in your future success. This might sound obvious, but it's important. The people you need to help your project, and the people you need to buy or use your project, will be able to sense your level of enthusiasm and dedication. In this sense, being a great

builder of side projects is like being a great entrepreneur.
You need a deep-seated conviction that you are doing the
right thing. One of the reasons Wetherell had the chutzpah to bypass the usual Google channels and convince
an engineer with root access to deploy Google Reader
on a server is that he was truly confident the product
could take off. Buchheit was so confident in AdSense that
he was willing to defy an order from Gmail's product
manager, Marissa Mayer. "I don't remember Marissa ever
liking [AdSense]," Buchheit told me, "[but] I wouldn't
have taken them down even if she did ask."

- **Go outside.** A great side project walks the line between
the host company's core competencies and outside technologies and ways of thinking that the company hasn't
embraced. It brings a piece of the outside world inside
the corporate walls. As such, it is wise to reach out to
the outside world repeatedly for feedback and inspiration. This could include a software, music, or art Hack
Day; it could also include a loosely structured forum like
BarCamp, which has been used as the basis for creative
workshops in tech, politics, health care, city planning,
and other fields.

You can get useful perspective on your project at any
event or meeting that puts you in touch with people
beyond your usual coworkers. Keller and his team didn't
realize Ad Hoc could be a viable permanent restaurant
until Yountville, California, locals started approaching
them on the street begging them not to shut it down.

The demoralized employees behind Flickr got a much-needed boost by demonstrating a very early version of their photo-sharing software at O'Reilly's Emerging Technology Conference. The Bronx Academy of Letters brought professional authors to its fund-raising board and into its classrooms to upgrade its students' educational experiences. Likewise, you can learn a lot by embracing outsiders.

- **Keep going, even if you have to turn.** Creating a successful product or organization is often a long and tough road, even if you've already got an entire company built up around you. It took Buchheit two and half years to launch Gmail. Off the Bus had nearly a year and a half to run before the election, and there were lessons all along the way for its leaders. Even relatively short periods of time can feel long when you're putting in intense hours, as Flickr's founders did with their fourteen-to-eighteen-hour days.

  But it's not enough to persist. You also have to be on the lookout for indications that you should change course. It took Michel a few months to admit to herself that she needed a journalist like Marc Cooper working by her side. It took financial desperation for Fake and Butterfield to realize that they should try to "pivot" their video game company around a new photo-sharing idea. It's possible that your own most promising future might require you to turn on a dime. So be ready to do just that.

LATE STAGE—GROWTH AND RESOLUTION

When your project reaches its later stages, you push up against the challenges of life inside a company built around some other idea. You need to grow to survive. You need resources to grow. You need smarts to make the most of your resources. And eventually you need to resolve your idea's future within the company if all of that energy and bother are to last.

- **Find patrons and allied projects.** When your project is in the advanced stages of development, it begins to bump up against problems that require not just the human capital of time and energy but the old-fashioned kind of capital. Gmail, for example, needed more hard drives and servers; Hack Day wanted to invite hundreds of geeks to camp overnight on its corporate campus; the Huffington Post needed to develop a kind of Web page that didn't exist in its publishing system. This is when you need friends in high places. I'm telling you this now, so you can cultivate these patrons *before* your project desperately needs their help. As you put together your side project, seek advice, counsel, and encouragement from trusted mentors and superiors within the organization, people you may be able to turn to later.

  You may also be able to get help from another project, particularly an officially favored project, by convincing the higher-ups that your project is crucial to the other's success. Recall how Wetherell was able to obtain some measure of official sanction when his politically weak Google Reader project was deemed to be a "dependency," or required subcomponent, of the "iGoogle" customizable home page project. This help from the iGoogle team made Google Reader possible.

- **Highlight investments that will benefit everyone.** One of the best ways to get your company to bet on your project is to convince your company it is not betting on your product. There are invariably techniques and technologies developed for a side project that end up having benefits for the entire organization, even if the side project is folded up and forgotten about. So show your bosses features, improvements, and technologies that have strong potential to be spun out to benefit the entire organization. They'll be much more inclined to provide resources to that sort of product development than to development tightly coupled to your personal vision.

  The Huffington Post's tech staff strongly resisted Michel and Cooper's insistent requests for a "big news page" where they could showcase their Iowa caucus coverage, a page that could be laid out like the HuffPo's front page or like its section pages but that was actually neither. After HuffPo tech relented, the big news page turned out to be a much bigger deal, being used hundreds of times by HuffPo proper versus just a handful by Off the Bus.

- **Bend over backward to make do with existing systems.** You are more likely to get resources if you're clearly pushing to the limit all the resources you've already got. Off the Bus never did get most of the tech it wanted, not even a simple Web form where writers could type in their articles directly. Instead, they ran almost everything off e-mail and a giant Excel spreadsheet. Buchheit begged spare hard drives and servers off other teams at Google. Flickr made do with tags rather than splurging on fancy image-recognition software. Even Keller, owner of two of the fanciest restaurants in the world, bought second-hand and pulled things from storage when it came time to furnish Ad Hoc.

- **Communicate constantly with the mother ship.** Side projects tend to be disruptive in nature, so giving your superiors frequent updates, particularly in your project's later stages, will help protect it from controversy. It is likewise a good idea to give colleagues in other groups frequent communiqués about anything you are doing that might impact them. Keeping up a constant flow of communication will help not only to smooth over bruised egos but to build political support for your project, laying the essential groundwork for when you want to graduate a 20 percent project into something bigger.

For all that's known about how to develop a successful side project, it is early yet in the spread of the 20 Percent Doctrine. All the time, we're seeing interesting new vehicles for tapping into workers' autonomous creativity. As I was finishing this book, National Public Radio began experimenting with what it called Serendipity Day, in which its tech employees got to spend a day working on whatever they wanted, with managers acting only to provide for them (a spare designer, say, or a room). Employees spent the afternoon beforehand prepping and the morning after presenting their work. "The energy level in the room just went through the roof," product strategy director Sarah Lumbard told Harvard's Nieman Journalism Lab. "And the biggest thing we heard from our team is, 'When are we doing this again?'"

Not long before Serendipity Day, a team at Condé Nast brought in a slew of outsiders—programmers, bloggers, tech executives, and other consultants—to form a "virtual start-up" within the luxury magazine conglomerate to create Gourmet Live, an iPad app that combined magazine-like content about food with the dynamics of a video game. After the outsiders left, the Condé Nast team continued their start-up-like mode of operation and created a side project called Idea Flight. Idea Flight has nothing to do with the magazine business; it's an iPad app designed to replace meeting handouts. It allows a meeting leader to choreograph the order in which documents show up within the app, preventing people from flipping ahead. The app also lets everyone in the meeting see the LinkedIn profiles of the other participants. After the meeting ends, the presentation is unlocked and participants can take it with them and page through it freely.

"What's just as compelling as the Idea Flight app is what it shows us about what's possible in big companies," wrote tech entrepreneur Anil Dash. "While it's a Condé Nast release, it's not based on any of their well-known magazine titles, it's a new brand that's aimed right at a new target audience of professional users."

More and more large organizations like NPR and Condé Nast are finding they can successfully inject the energy and creative freedom of start-ups into their own teams using 20 Percent Doctrine principles. And why couldn't they? If a massive urban school district can devolve creative freedom, certainly they can, too. If a famously meticulous, fifty-six-year-old chef can learn the art of the hack, then they can as well. If some of Silicon Valley's most hard-core nerds can turn a bit punk rock, surely they can follow their lead. As more and more 20 Percent Doctrine projects succeed, more people will try to follow their examples, and we should end up with more innovation, creativity, emotional touchpoints, and indeed more humanity in the modern workplace. And that will be a true blessing.

BIBLIOGRAPHY

INTRODUCTION

Beda, Joe. "Google 20% Time." EightyPercent.net, Mar. 24, 2005.

Board of Governors of the Federal Reserve System. "Flow of Funds Accounts of the United States." Sept. 2011.

Buchheit, Paul. Interviews.

Conference Board. "U.S. Job Satisfaction at Lowest Level in Two Decades." conference-board.org, Jan. 5, 2010.

Dash, Anil. "The Virtual Start-up: Taking Flight." anil. dashes.com, June 22, 2011.

Dougherty, Dale. Talk: "We Are Makers." TED conference, Jan. 2011.

Fried, Ina. "Google+ Guru Bradley Horowitz on Products, Platforms and That Pesky Memo." All Things D, Oct. 20, 2011.

Hamel, Gary. *The Future of Management*. Harvard Business School Press, 2007.

Kretkowski, Paul D. "The 15 Percent Solution." *Wired*, Jan. 23, 1998.

Levy, Steven. *In the Plex*. Simon & Schuster, 2011.

Na, Piaw. Interviews.

Page, Larry. Talk: "Sergey Brin and Larry Page on Google." TED conference, Feb. 2004.

3M Company. *A Century of Innovation: The 3M Story*. 3M Company, 2002.

Tsotsis, Alexia. "Google's '20 Percent Time' Will Survive the Death of Google Labs." *TechCrunch*, July 20, 2011.

U.S. Bureau of Economic Analysis. "Real Private Fixed Investment in Equipment and Software by Type, Chained Dollars." Oct. 2011.

———. "Real Private Fixed Investment in Structures by Type, Chained Dollars." Oct. 2011.

U.S. Bureau of Labor Statistics. "Labor Force Statistics from the Current Population Survey." Oct. 2011.

U.S. Congressional Budget Office. "The Budget and Economic Outlook: An Update." Aug. 2011.

Wetherell, Chris. Interview.

CHAPTER 1: Scratching Your Own Itch

Buchheit, Paul. Interviews.

———. "The Most Important Thing to Understand About New Products and Start-ups." paulbuchheit.blogspot.com, Feb. 17, 2008.

———. Talk: "Paul Buchheit at Start-up School 08." Y Combinator, Apr. 2008.

———. "Overnight Success Takes a Long Time." paulbuchheit.blogspot.com, Jan. 4, 2009.

———. "Communicating with Code." paulbuchheit
.blogspot.com, Jan. 22, 2009.

Hamel, Gary. *The Future of Management*. Harvard Business
School Press, 2007.

Katdare, Kaustubh. "Paul Buchheit—Creator of Gmail,
AdSense & FriendFeed." CrazyEngineers.com, Mar. 1,
2009.

Liu, Min. "Marissa Mayer, VP of Search Products and User
Experience at Google." iinnovate podcast, Stanford University, Aug. 31, 2007.

Livingston, Jessica. *Founders at Work*. Apress, 2007.

Na, Piaw. Interview.

Spolsky, Joel. "Controlling Your Environment Makes You
Happy." JoelOnSoftware.com, Apr. 2, 2010.

Wetherell, Chris. Interview.

CHAPTER 2: 20 Percent on the Cheap

Chafkin, Max. "Anything Could Happen." *Inc.*, Mar. 1,
2008.

Fake, Caterina. Interviews.

———. "Working Hard Is Overrated." Caterina.net, Sept.
25, 2009.

Hicks, Matthew. "Online Collaboration Born from Multi-
player Game." eWeek.com, Feb. 12, 2004.

Kirkpatrick, David. "Twitter Was Act One." *Vanity Fair*,
Apr. 2011.

Livingston, Jessica. *Founders at Work*. Apress, 2007.

Ludicorp. "Flickr Launches!" ludicorp.com, Feb. 20, 2004.

Malik, Om. "Odeo RIP, Hello Obvious Corp." GigaOm
.com, Oct. 25, 2006.

Schofield, Jack. "Let's Be Friendsters." *Guardian*, Feb. 19, 2004.

Williams, Ev. "The Birth of Obvious Corp." evhead.com, Oct. 25, 2006.

CHAPTER 3: The Rise of Hack Day

Cannon-Brookes, Mike. Interview.

———. "The Inaugural 'FedEx Day'—Atlassian Meets Google's 20%." blogs.atlassian.com, Apr. 22, 2005.

Dickerson, Chad. Interviews.

———. "Blown Away (Again) by Hack Day." blog.chad dickerson.com, Mar. 26, 2006.

———. "Yahoo! Hack Day Tomorrow, and Some of My Inspirations." blog.chaddickerson.com, June 14, 2006.

———. "Loads of New Stuff from Yahoo! Developer Network for Open Hack Day." blog.chaddickerson.com, Oct. 1, 2006.

———. "Yahoo! Open Hack Day: How It All Came Together." blog.chaddickerson.com, Oct. 3, 2006.

Hoffman, Havi. Interviews.

———. "The History of Hack Day." YDN Blog, June 14, 2007.

———. "A Very Personal Ramble Down Hackday Memory Lane." YDN Blog, May 8, 2009.

Horowitz, Bradley. Interviews.

Kakwan, Mo. Interview.

———. "Funny Guy Mo on Yahoo! Hack Day '06—Saved by Patrick Stewart." Pulse2.com, Oct. 3, 2006.

Kennedy, Ryan. "Yahoo! Open Hack Day Wrap-up." Ryan Kennedy's Blog, Oct. 2, 2006.

Korula, Tarikh. Interview.

Kraus, Joe. "JotSpot Inaugural Hackathon." JotSpot Blog, May 9, 2005.

Mason, Hilary. Interview.

McAlister, Matt. "Top 10 Reasons Why Hack Day Rocks." mattmcalister.com, Mar. 26, 2006.

Mernit, Susan. "HackDay: Thoughts on How Yahoo Got There and What It All Means." SusanMernit.com, Oct. 1, 2006.

Metcalfe, Ben. "Yahoo! Hack Day Was Off the Hook." ben-metcalfe.com, Oct. 3, 2006.

Norton, Ken. Interview.

Raffel, Daniel. Interviews.

Rotenstein, John. "Atlassian's 20% Time Now Out of Beta." blogs.atlassian.com, Mar. 23, 2009.

Silvers, Jon. "FedEx Day in the Wild." blogs.atlassian.com, Nov. 12, 2010.

Weinberg, Gabriel. "Rapid Prototyping as Burnout Antidote." gabrielweinberg.com, Aug. 24, 2010.

Zawodny, Jeremy. Interviews.

———. "Yahoo's First Hack Day: What a Blast!" jeremy.zawodny.com, Dec. 9, 2005.

CHAPTER 4: A Side Project School Rises in the Bronx

Bernstein, Toni. Interview.

Brill, Steven. "The Rubber Room." *The New Yorker*, Aug. 31, 2009.

———. "The School Reform Deniers." Reuters, Aug. 21, 2011.

Bronx Academy of Letters. "History." bronxletters.com, accessed March 27, 2011.

Cramer, Philissa, and Elizabeth Green. "Joel Klein's Bumpy Learning Curve on the Path to Radical Change." GothamSchools.org, Nov. 10, 2010.

Goldstein, Dana. "Joel Klein's Sad and Cynical *Atlantic* Essay." danagoldstein.net, May 12, 2011.

Gootman, Elissa. "The New Team: Joel I. Klein." *New York Times*, Nov. 9, 2008.

Haddad, Anne. "The Write Stuff: The Bronx Academy of Letters Puts Pen to Pupil." UrbaniteBaltimore.com, Aug. 1, 2005.

Hamilton, Sarah. "Mayor Villaraigosa Names Joan Sullivan Deputy Mayor of Education." mayor.lacity.org, Dec. 21, 2009.

Hernandez, Javier C. "Departing Schools Chief: 'We Weren't Bold Enough.'" *New York Times*, Dec. 24, 2010.

Hoffman, Jan. "PUBLIC LIVES; A Traveler Showing Students a Different Path." *New York Times*, Oct. 21, 2003.

Hurst, Mark. "Joan Sullivan (follow-up)." gelconference.com, June 2009.

Klein, Joel. Interview.

———. "The Failure of American Schools." *The Atlantic*, June 2011.

Lemann, Nicholas. "Comment: Schoolwork." *New Yorker*, Sept. 27, 2010.

Llanos, Connie. "Can She Bring Bronx Success to L.A. Schools?" *Los Angeles Daily News*, Dec. 20, 2009.

New York City Department of Education. "Elementary,

Middle, High, and Schools for Transfer Students Schools Receiving 2006/07 Progress Report Grades." Apr. 7, 2008.

Nocera, Joe. "Lesson Plan from a Departing Schools Chief." *New York Times*, Nov. 12, 2010.

Otterman, Sharon, and Jennifer Medina. "New York Schools Chancellor Ends 8-Year Run." *New York Times*, Nov. 9, 2010.

Ravitch, Diane. "School 'Reform': A Failing Grade." *New York Review of Books*, Sept. 29, 2011.

Rein, Rich. "Feminist Pryde Brown Finds House-Husband Dan Sullivan a 'Wonderful Mother' of Ten." *People*, Oct. 13, 1975.

Sivack, Emily, Katie DeRogatis, Manuel Rosaldo, Rebecca Robinson, Stuart Harmon, and Ted Fisher. "Back-to-School Special! Joan Sullivan on the Importance of Effective Communication." dowser.org, Sept. 1, 2010.

Sullivan, Joan. Interviews.

———. *An American Voter: My Love Affair with Presidential Politics*. Bloomsbury USA, 2002.

———. Talk. Gel Conference, May 2009.

———. Talk: "Ms. Sullivan Farewell." Bronx Academy of Letters, Jan. 2010.

Zoepf, Katherine. "Small Bronx High School Now a Model for Others." *New York Times*, Sept. 19, 2003.

CHAPTER 5: The Huffington Post Brings 20 Percent to the Masses

Arnoldy, Ben. "Army of Average Joes Culls Through

Candidates' Files, Bios." *Christian Science Monitor*, Oct. 17, 2007.

Berlind, David. "Publicly Selected and Funded Investigative Reporting: Can It Work?" ZDNet, July 25, 2006.

Bogut, Jennifer. Interview.

Carr, David. "In Politics, the Gaffe Goes Viral." *New York Times*, Apr. 21, 2008.

Cooper, Marc. Interviews.

———. "Closed to Press—Not Off the Record." marccooper.com, Apr. 16, 2008.

Fowler, Mayhill. Interviews.

———. "Obama: No Surprise That Hard-Pressed Pennsylvanians Turn Bitter." Huffington Post, Apr. 11, 2008.

———. "Bill Clinton: Purdum a 'Sleazy' 'Slimy' 'Scumbag.'" Huffington Post, June 2, 2008.

———. *Notes from a Clueless Journalist: Media, Bias and the Great Election of 2008.* 2010.

———. "Why I Left The Huffington Post." mayhillfowler.com, Sept. 25, 2010.

Halloran, Liz. "Media Takes: Giving the 'Smart Mob' a Voice in the Media." *US News and World Report*, July 26, 2006.

Healy, Patrick. "Obama's 2nd-Quarter Foray in New York." *New York Times*, Mar. 21, 2007.

Hova, Ethan, and Thomas Edsall. "Romney Buys Conservatives." Huffington Post, July 26, 2007.

Howe, Jeff. "Did Assignment Zero Fail? A Look Back, and Lessons Learned." Wired.com, July 16, 2007.

Kalter, Lindsay. "A Campaign Trail Neophyte Who

Scooped the Pros." *American Journalism Review*, Oct. 2008.

Michel, Amanda. Interviews.

———. "Get Off the Bus: The Future of Pro-Am Journalism; OffTheBus." *Columbia Journalism Review*, Mar. 2009.

Morgan, Betsy. Interview.

Rainey, James. Interview.

Rosen, Jay. Interviews.

———. "Introducing NewAssignment.Net." PressThink, July 25, 2006.

———. "Assignment Zero Lands. OffTheBus Launches. Lessons Fly." PressThink, June 20, 2007.

———. "What I Learned from Assignment Zero." PressThink, Oct. 9, 2007.

———. "Some Problems with NewAssignment.Net." PressThink, July 28, 2009.

Rosenberg, Scott. "NewAssignment.Net: New-Model Journalism." Scott Rosenberg's WordYard, July 25, 2006.

———. "Rosen on NewAssignment.Net: It's Made of Editors." Scott Rosenberg's WordYard, July 28, 2006.

Seelye, Katherine Q. "A New Campaign Media Entry." *New York Times*, May 18, 2007.

———. "The Women Behind the Scenes." *New York Times*, Oct. 24, 2007.

———. "Blogger Is Surprised by Uproar over Obama Story, but Not Bitter." *New York Times*, Apr. 14, 2008.

———. "Off the Bus, but Growing Thousands Strong." *New York Times*, July 23, 2008.

———. "Citizen-Journalism Project Gains a Voice in the Campaign." *New York Times*, July 25, 2008.

Shirky, Clay. Interview.

Smith, Ben. Interview.

Steinberg, Jacques. "For New Journalists, All Bets, but Not Mikes, Are Off." *New York Times*, June 8, 2008.

Teachout, Zephyr, and Thomas Streeter. *Mousepads, Shoe Leather, and Hope: Lessons from the Howard Dean Campaign for the Future of Internet Politics.* Paradigm Publishers, 2007.

Teo, Dawn. Interview.

Tomasic, John. Interview.

Treul, Dan. Interview.

CHAPTER 6: How a Top Chef Started Over

Bauer, Michael. Interviews.

———. "An Ad Hoc Look at Ad Hoc." *San Francisco Chronicle*, Sept. 29, 2006.

———. "Duo Reunites in Wine Country." *San Francisco Chronicle*, Oct. 25, 2006.

———. "Keller's Ad Hoc Elevates Rustic, Family-Style Dining." *San Francisco Chronicle*, Nov. 26, 2006.

———. "Ad Hoc to Become Permanent." *San Francisco Chronicle*, Jan. 17, 2007.

Berne, Amanda, Kim Severson, Stephanie Dimiceli, Carol Ness, and Karola Saekel. "What's New." *San Francisco Chronicle*, Sept. 1, 2004.

———. "Keller Expands Empire." *San Francisco Chronicle*, Apr. 5, 2006.

———. "Cozmo's Grill in the Marina to Get an Upscale Makeover." *San Francisco Chronicle*, May 24, 2006.

———. "New Chef, New Menu for Mecca." *San Francisco*

Chronicle, July 12, 2006.

Cerciello, Jeffrey. Interview.

Cruz, Dave. Interview.

Finz, Stacy. "Keller Right-Hand Man Jeffrey Cerciello Going Out on His Own." *San Francisco Chronicle*, Jan. 28, 2010.

Keefer, Kristine. Interviews.

Keller, Thomas. Interview.

————. *Ad Hoc at Home*. Artisan, 2009.

————. Talk. Commonwealth Club, Sept. 30, 2010.

McGeehon, Allison. Interview.

Mustich, James. "Table Talk with Thomas Keller." barnes andnoblereview.com, Nov. 24, 2009.

Raffel, Daniel. Interviews.

Ragone, Gina LaVecchia. "Casual Gets Classy." *Restaurant Hospitality*, May 1, 2008.

Ruhlman, Michael. *The Soul of a Chef.* Penguin Group, 2001.

Walden, GraceAnn. "Marc Rasic to Head Up Kitchen at Fringale." *San Francisco Chronicle*, Apr. 21, 2004.

Wolf, Clark. Interview.

CONCLUSION

Dash, Anil. "The Virtual Start-up: Taking Flight." dashes .com, June 22, 2011.

Phelps, Andrew. "NPR Tries Something New: A Day to Let Managers Step Away and Developers Play." nieman lab.org, Aug. 23, 2011.

INDEX

ABOUT THE AUTHOR

Ryan Tate is the technology gossip blogger for Gawker
.com and a veteran business journalist whose posts are read
2.5 million times by 700,000 people per month. He began his
career writing for *Upside*, the first magazine to focus on the
intersection of business and technology. He then went on to
write and report for Business 2.0 magazine, the *Contra Costa
Times* and the *San Francisco Business Times*. He lives in the San
Francisco Bay Area with his wife and two cats.